Sukhoi Su-27 'Flanker'

Aerospace SuperProfile

Sukhoi Su-27 'Flanker'

including Su-30 to Su-35

Jon Lake

WORLD AIR POWER JOURNAL

Aerospace Publishing Ltd
Airtime Publishing Inc.

Published by
Aerospace Publishing Ltd
179 Dalling Road
London W6 0ES
England

Published under licence in USA
and Canada by
AIRtime Publishing Inc.
10 Bay Street
Westport, CT 06880
USA

Distributed in the UK,
Commonwealth and Europe by
Airlife Publishing Ltd
101 Longden Road
Shrewsbury SY3 9EB
England
Tel: 0743 235651
Fax: 0743 232944

US and Canadian readers wishing to order by mail, please contact AIRtime Publishing Inc. at (203) 226-3580. The publishers also welcome inquiries from model and hobby stores.

First published 1994

ISBN (Aerospace): 1 874023 53 0
ISBN (AIRtime): 1-880588-12-9

Publisher: Stan Morse
Managing Editor: David Donald
Sub Editor: Karen Leverington
Editorial Assistant: Tim Senior
Design: Barry Savage
Robert Hewson

Artists: Mike Badrocke
Keith Fretwell
Mark Styling

Origination by Imago Publishing Ltd

Printed in Singapore

The author and editors would like to thank the following individuals for their invaluable assistance: Mr Mikhail P. Simonov, General Vladimir Ilyushin, Mr Victor Pugachev, Mr Oleg Tsoi, Mr Yevgeni Frolov, Mr Nikolai Nikitin, Mr Igor P. Emelianov, Mr Mikhail Pougasyin and Mr Avramenko of the Sukhoi Design Bureau. Thanks are also due to Mr Boris Rybak and Mr Sergei Skrynnikov of Avia Data, and to Mr John Farley for his insights, and finally to 'the late' Mr Mark Styling for his excellent artwork and plans, whose scrupulous preparation revealed many new facts. Any errors and omissions are the author's.

Much of the material in this book has been published previously in *World Air Power Journal* Volume 15.

CONTENTS

Sukhoi Su-27 'FLANKER' & Su-30, Su-33, Su-35

Although to Western fighter pilots virtually every enemy aircraft is generically known as 'a MiG', the latest products of the well known Mikoyan Design Bureau are steadily being overshadowed by fighters produced by their great rival, Sukhoi, which previously specialised in heavyweight interceptors and lumbering fighter-bombers. One aircraft in particular is responsible for the Sukhoi OKB's dramatic change in fortunes: the Su-27, known to NATO as 'Flanker'. Air show appearances have demonstrated an almost unbelieveable level of agility and an ability to perform manoeuvres that no Western fighter can emulate, while record-breaking flights speak volumes for the aircraft's incredibly high performance and ultra-long range. Routine Cold War encounters showed Western pilots an aircraft which regularly bristled with as many as 10 advanced air-to-air missiles, and whose bulbous radome clearly contained an advanced long-range pulse-Doppler radar, with genuine look-down/shoot-down capability. It seems little wonder that the Su-27 has been selected as the cornerstone around which the Russian air forces will enter the new millennium.

Main picture: A PVO 'Flanker' lands, its tyres leaving a puff of smoke. The Su-27 is a huge aircraft for a single-seat fighter, larger even than America's broadly equivalent F-15.

Right: A pair of Su-27s in flight. Soviet fighter tactics began to change with the introduction of the MiG-29 and Su-27, with a corresponding reduction in the traditional reliance on tight GCI control and a move towards greater flexibility and more reactive tactics.

Above: The first of the 'Flankers'. The T-10 prototype pictured at the Flight Research Centre at Zhukovsky at about the time of its first flight, with camera calibration markings and without the distinctive anti-flutter weights added later in the flight test programme.

Right: Pilot of the T-10 on its first flight was General Vladimir Ilyushin (son of the famous designer), who continues to act as a consultant to, and ambassador for, the Sukhoi OKB, and is still one of the great characters of Russian aviation.

Below: The first prototype wore an attractive two-tone light grey/blue colour scheme. Pictures of the aircraft in flight are extremely rare, but give an impression of the very different wing planform, and other discontinued features.

Even today, the Su-27 is an enigma. Dazzling air show routines and a clutch of world records (snatched from the rival F-15) speak for an incredible level of performance and agility, while huge internal fuel capacity gives the aircraft an enormous range. The type has been selected as the multi-role cornerstone of the Russian air force into the next century, eclipsing all rivals. Lockheed YF-22 project personnel, writing in their own company magazine, referred to the aircraft thus: "The Russians are hot fighter jocks and the Su-27 and MiG-29 are sportier than anything we have in the inventory . . . but the F-22 will have better manoeuvrability than the Su-27, which is Top Gun at the moment." In Europe, supporters of the European Fighter Aircraft inevitably use the Su-27, or a fictitious 'Su-27 with X number of years development' as their baseline threat aircraft to explain why Europe's most advanced combat aircraft is essential.

The aircraft everyone is talking about had a difficult birth and a disastrous early history, and the weapons system and radar are still widely regarded as being primitive and of limited effectiveness. There is no shortage of admirers or detractors of the Su-27, and it remains difficult to discern the truth – is the aircraft an over-rated mediocrity or a multi-talented, enormously capable star?

When the Cold War ended, and the former Soviet Union split asunder, things changed overnight for the military, which immediately lost its unlimited funding and privileged status. The shock was no less severe in the aviation industry, since production of most military aircraft was halted or slashed, and countless new projects were cancelled. The Russian air force decided as an economy measure to move towards standardisation on a single tactical aircraft type. The aircraft they chose was the Su-27 'Flanker'.

This decision clearly demonstrated the success and popularity of the aircraft, and was a testament to its versatility and potential for further development but, perhaps more interestingly, it showed the extent to which the Sukhoi OKB (Design Bureau), under the charismatic leadership of Mikhail Petrovich Simonov, had gained a political ascendancy over its rivals. Thus, while the Su-27 has been selected as the 'backbone' aircraft with which the Russian air force will enter the new millennium, there are already impotent mutterings of anger and discontent from disgruntled rival 'firms' and from many senior air force officers who acknowledge the Su-27's capability as an interceptor, but who correctly and realistically point to its enormous price tag, its lack of suitability for the tactical air superiority fighter role, and to its shortcomings as a potential carrier-based multi-role fighter or land-based tactical bomber.

Look-down/shoot-down

When the aircraft was conceived, few would have dared predict the scale of its eventual success, and its early history was so disastrous that cancellation of the entire project seemed a real possibility on several separate occasions. The Su-27 was conceived during 1969, after the Sukhoi OKB won a design contract to design a long-range interceptor to replace the Tu-128 'Fiddler', Su-15 'Flagon' and Yak-28P 'Firebar' in IA-PVO service. Current OKB Designer General Simonov has since commented that "we won, but as so often happens, it was decided to adopt the losing aircraft as well!" This statement has been taken as being an indication that the Su-27 and MiG-31 were designed as competitors, and that the latter aircraft was also adopted as a low-risk 'insurance policy' and stop-gap. From an early stage, it was decided that the new Sukhoi aircraft would have a limited Frontal Aviation role as a long-range escort fighter for strike aircraft like the Su-24 'Fencer' and as a complement to Mikoyan's MiG-29, destroying high-value assets like tankers and AWACS platforms far beyond the front line, while the MiG-29 concentrated on fighters and fighter-bombers.

The growing importance of low-level penetration tactics dictated that the new fighter should be capable of look-down/shoot-down intercepts, while the increasing use of stand-off weapons such as cruise missiles made it necessary to intercept targets at very long range (preferably before their weapons could be launched) and to be capable of intercepting low-flying missiles. As if this requirement was not difficult enough, Sukhoi was instructed that the new fighter should be capable of destroying 'enemy fighter aircraft which protect the target zone', which was taken as a directive that the new fighter should be able to better the new American F-15 in air-to-air combat.

The design team for the new fighter was led by Yevgeny Ivanov, with Oleg Samolovich as his deputy and Designer General Pavel Osipovich Sukhoi giving the benefit of his considerable experience. Sukhoi died in 1975, and was replaced by Simonov, but no change was made to the design team. Samolovich has stated that after two years of preliminary work, the basic layout of the aircraft was drawn up over a single weekend (to avoid interruptions) by only three men, one of whom, Vladimir Antonov, worked on the project as part of his post-graduate university studies. Another (possibly apocryphal) story from the early days relates that in order to reduce weight, Ivanov designed the aircraft to 90 per cent of ultimate design load then strengthened only those areas shown to be deficient by static testing.

The first prototype, given the bureau designation T-10-1, made its maiden flight on 20 May 1977 at Zhukhovsky, in the hands of Vladimir Ilyushin, the bureau chief test pilot, whose CV covered 143 aircraft types, including the B-25 Mitchell, Northrop F-5E and Cessna A-37, as well as several Sikorsky helicopters. The aircraft was powered by AL-21F-3 engines, as used by the Su-17, with the afterburner nozzles completely enclosed within the rear fuselage, like those of the Su-24 'Fencer'. Spotted at Zhukhovsky (then erroneously referred to by Western intelligence agencies as Ramenskoye) by a US satellite, the aircraft was allocated the provisional reporting name 'RAM-J'. A handful of these images were eventually seen by the press, but the quality of the released images was so poor that little could be inferred about the new fighter. One well known and distinguished analyst was even convinced that he could see variable geometry wings. This prototype aircraft later provided the Western aviation press with its first useful glimpse of the Su-27 in 1985, when stills from a TV documentary about the Sukhoi OKB were released, and the machine can now be seen in the air forces' museum at Monino, near Moscow.

Familiar configuration

The aircraft was of typical late 1960s/early 1970s configuration, with twin vertical tailfins, widely spaced underslung engines and a blended wing/forebody, with some features reminiscent of some aspects of the rival US F-15 and F-14. Since Western analysts at that time believed that Soviet

Below: The West's first view of the Su-27 was provided by a 10-second clip on Soviet TV during a documentary about Sukhoi. This showed the T-10-1 landing and taking off, perhaps on its first flight.

Left: The only other T-10 prototype photograph seen in the West shows an aircraft apparently coded 51, seen here.

The first T-10 ended its days in the impressive air forces museum collection at Monino, heading a row of Sukhoi OKB fighters and prototypes. The aircraft has had primitive anti-flutter weights added to the leading edges of the tailfins, wingtips and tailerons, and its camouflage has been faded and bleached by summer sun and winter snow.

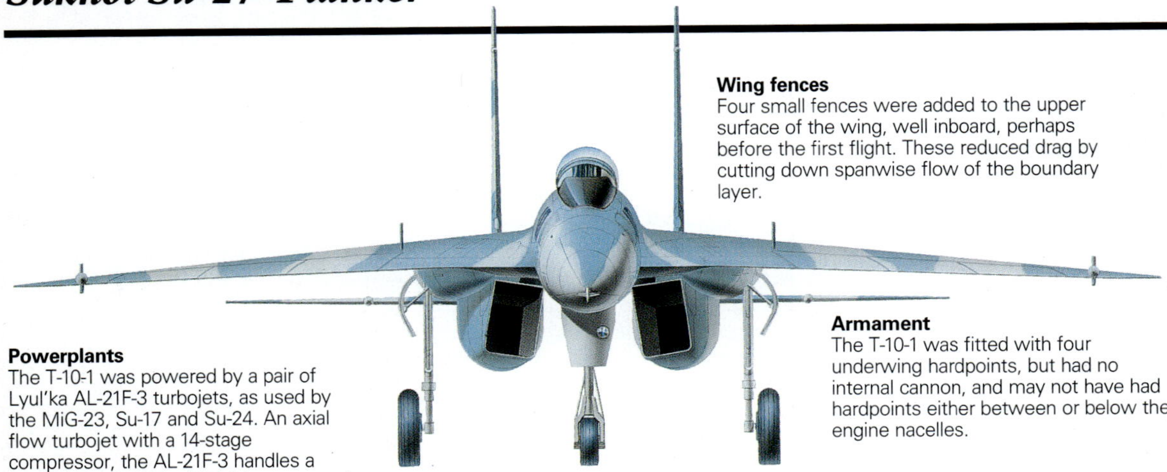

Wing fences
Four small fences were added to the upper surface of the wing, well inboard, perhaps before the first flight. These reduced drag by cutting down spanwise flow of the boundary layer.

Radar
The T-10s were ready long before their intended radar, and were therefore completed with empty metal nosecones of simple conical shape. Ballast was fitted to maintain the centre of gravity.

Powerplants
The T-10-1 was powered by a pair of Lyul'ka AL-21F-3 turbojets, as used by the MiG-23, Su-17 and Su-24. An axial flow turbojet with a 14-stage compressor, the AL-21F-3 handles a mass flow of 104 kg (229 lb) per second and has a pressure ratio of 14.75. The engine produces 76.5 kN (17,200 lb st) in full military power (8,400 rpm) and 110.5 kN (24,800 lb st) in full burner.

Armament
The T-10-1 was fitted with four underwing hardpoints, but had no internal cannon, and may not have had hardpoints either between or below the engine nacelles.

Wing planform
The original T-10 prototypes had a gracefully curving wingtip, which was square-cropped and fitted with a missile launch rail-cum-flutter weight on production aircraft.

Sukhoi T-10-1

The first prototype T-10, forerunner of the Su-27, is shown late in its life. The aircraft made a long and valuable contribution to the flight test programme before being retired to the air forces museum at Monino, just outside Moscow. The aircraft was camouflaged overall in two tones of grey-blue, the disruptive pattern continuing on to the lower surfaces.

Afterburner
The fully variable afterburner nozzles are fully enclosed in the rear fuselage, as on the Su-24, and can be used over the whole power range from flight idle to maximum power, giving smooth modulated increases in power output.

Anti-flutter weights
The T-10-1 was fitted with prominent and rather crude leading-edge spikes on the vertical tailfins, the horizontal tail surfaces and the wingtips, some time after the first flight. These were intended to alleviate some of the original aircraft's flutter problems. In the end, a total aerodynamic redesign proved necessary. The T-10-1 retains its spike-like anti-flutter weights to this day.

Cockpit
The T-10s had a simple wraparound windscreen and a one-piece bubble canopy, both of which had to be reshaped and strengthened on the production Su-27. The priority of giving the pilot a good, unobstructed all-round view was apparent even at this early stage.

engineers were both backward and incapable of any original thought, this led inevitably to accusations that Sukhoi had copied one or other of the US aircraft. The wing was very clean, with a drooping leading edge but no leading-edge slats and no anti-flutter weights, and with conventional outboard ailerons and inboard flaps. The root was swept at about 80°, and the main part of the leading edge at 44° out to the gracefully curving tip. Four small fences were added on the inboard panels, perhaps before the first flight. The twin fins were uncanted and were mounted on top of the engine nacelles, just outboard of the centreline. Box section beams on the sides of the nacelles carried the slab tailerons. The main undercarriage units were mounted in the wingroots, retracting forward and swivelling through 90° to lie horizontally in the wing. Large forward undercarriage doors, hinged on their leading edges, acted as airbrakes, à la Folland Gnat. The tall nose gear was located well forward, below the windscreen, retracting aft.

The design team, drawing on extensive work carried out by the Central Aerodynamics Institute, TsAGI, chose to use what the Russians call an 'integrated airframe' in which forebody and wing are blended together to form, in effect, a single, unified lifting body. This blending (also used on the American F-16) gives a smaller wetted area (and thus lower drag) and greater internal volume for fuel and avionics. The configuration allowed a smooth change in cross-sectional area, even at the canopy and air intakes, significantly reducing wave drag. The Su-27's very high internal fuel capacity is partly a result of this, but mainly as a result of the fighter's sheer size.

Low-slung nacelles

The engines were housed in low-slung, widely separated nacelles, leaving a significant tunnel between them, suitable for low-drag, low radar-signature stores carriage. The engines were separated to avoid the chance of damage to one resulting in damage to the other – a significant risk unless engines are widely spaced or separated by an armoured titanium 'keel'. Separate, widely spaced intakes allow simpler, 'straight-through' intake ducts, which are easier to design and more efficient, and which are more effective when the aircraft is sideslipping. Their underslung location is superior at high angles of attack. The intakes are separated from the underside of the fuselage/wing lifting body by a narrow gap, making the top of the intake effectively a splitter plate which removes sluggish boundary layer air. Boundary layer is also removed via tiny perforations in one of the three intake ramp sections. These are fully variable to alter intake area and angle, and thereby to control shock wave formation. They give the Su-27 its Mach 2 performance capability.

When Mikoyan's MiG-29 prototype was revealed, it

Norwegian air force F-16s began encountering Su-27s in early 1987, these aircraft usually being armed with six AA-10 'Alamos' but with wingtip and outboard underwing pylons empty.

Left: Early production Su-27s had a simple tailboom, with strakes on either side rather than the box-like fairings which on later aircraft house chaff/ flare dispensers.

Below: Early Su-27s retained small anti-flutter weights on the leading edge of each tailfin.

***Above:** The traditional 'sunburst' air forces flag is lowered at a Frontal Aviation 'Flanker' base at the end of the day. In the background an armed Su-27 waits in front of its shelter.*

***Right:** A g-suited pilot studies his briefing notes before climbing the ladder into the cockpit of his Su-27. Most Su-27 pilots wear the new lightweight Soviet flying helmet, which is distinguished by the row of holes across the top.*

could be seen to have a similar overall configuration, with twin fins, widely spaced engines and a blended wing/forward fuselage incorporating prominent leading-edge root extensions. This gave rise to inevitable accusation and counter-accusation that one bureau had copied the other's design. In fact no copying went on, the similarities in overall configuration being the inevitable result of common solutions being found for common problems and of common access to the research work of TsAGI and other research institutes. Interestingly, the changes to the Sukhoi prototype to bring it to the eventual production configuration made the aircraft more similar to the MiG-29 in appearance, with more widely spaced tailfins on booms beside the engine nacelles.

Even more galling to the two Russian design bureaux than accusations that they had copied one another was the chorus of accusations that they had copied elements of the various contemporary Western fighters. The twin fins were inevitably cited to have been 'ripped off' from the F-14, F-15 or YF-17, the widely-spaced engines from the F-14, the blended fuselage from the F-14 or F-16, and other features from one or other of the US fighters. For a nation which had put the first vehicle, animal and then man into space, and the nation whose aircraft industry had produced countless record-breaking aircraft, such misinformed comment was an unwelcome and unwarranted insult. "Just because you can see your neighbour toiling in his field doesn't mean you don't have to toil just as hard in your own," was a saying used frequently by irritated Russian designers.

Prototype crashes

The first and second prototypes were built by the OKB itself, in its Moscow 'workshop', albeit using wings and tails from the Komsomolsk-na-Amur production plant. The second prototype reportedly incorporated some improvements, including a flattened leading edge with moveable slats, canted tailfins and, according to some sources, was the first T-10 with the full standard fly-by-wire control system (originally developed for the T-4/Su-100, which was claimed by Sukhoi to have been the world's first operational FBW aircraft). It also had an extra tonne (2,204 lb) of internal fuel by comparison with the first aircraft's 9-tonne (19,841-lb) capacity. The T-10-2 was lost after a control system malfunction, which led to severe resonance. Yevgeny Soloviev was killed when he ejected outside seat parameters. The next two prototypes, T-10-3 and T-10-4, were also built by the bureau, but these were powered by the definitive production standard AL-31F (albeit with underslung accessories and gearboxes). T-10-3 made its maiden flight on 23 August 1979, and was followed by T-10-4 on 31 October. Five further prototypes were built by the production plant at Komsomolsk (T-10-5, T-10-6, T-10-9, T-10-10 and T-10-11), but these were powered by the AL-21F.

As the accidents were rocking the programme, information about the new US F-15 began to flood in, and it became clear that the T-10, which was failing to meet its own performance requirements, would be no match for the American fighter. This was caused by higher-than-expected drag figures, a performance shortfall from the engines, excessive specific fuel consumption figures and the excess weight of the newly developed avionics systems, which, since they were mainly fitted in the nose, also tended to in-

Inset left: A pair of Su-27s blasts off for an intercept mission. FOD protection screens in the intakes allow pairs take-offs even on rough or dirt strips.

Left: Two Su-27s pull contrails as they cruise high above the tundra. Tight formations are for photography only, even in Russia. Tactically, a much looser battle formation would be used.

crease the longitudinal stability of the aircraft. The aircraft also suffered from flutter problems, and these necessitated the provision of anti-flutter weights on the leading edges of the tailfins, tailplanes and wings, and the removal of one pair of overwing fences. It was clear that to meet its original requirement the new fighter would need to be subjected to a major redesign, and Sukhoi received permission to undertake this on condition that output of the Su-25 attack aircraft would not be affected.

Accordingly, the next two prototypes under construction at the OKB's Moscow facility, T-10-7 and T-10-8, were completed to a completely new standard, which was claimed by the OKB to be an 'entirely new aircraft' retaining only the 'T-10 designation, ejection seat and mainwheels'. The redesign was personally supervised by Mikhail Simonov, who reportedly came up with the new designation T-10S (T-10 Simonov) for the revised design. The two prototypes thus became T-10S-1 and T-10S-2. Even after work began on the two redesigned aircraft, Komsomolsk continued working on T-10 prototypes to the original configuration, for use as equipment and avionics testbeds. Some sources suggest that some 20 original-configuration T-10s were produced, but little evidence can be found to support this contention, and it seems that only nine flew.

The new aircraft was not an entirely 'clean sheet of paper' design, but it did represent a very major redesign. The key to the redesign was an entirely new wing. The LERXes were improved to give more lift (thereby helping to destabilise the heavier, equipment-packed nose) and the wing lost its curved tips, replacing these with massive flutter weights which doubled as wingtip missile launch rails. The ailerons (which had suffered from reversal problems because of the flexibility of the wing) and the original flaps were deleted and replaced by inboard flaperons. Less obviously, but no less importantly, the fuselage was extensively redesigned. Changes to the nose and forward fuselage were the most obvious, with a more capacious radome and reduced forward fuselage cross-section, but with increased cross-sectional area and less height immediately aft of the cabin. A GSh-30-1 cannon was fitted in the starboard wingroot, the same weapon as is used by the rival MiG-29. Designed by the OKB led by V. P. Gryazev and A. G. Shipunov, the cannon is used in conjunction with the laser rangefinder and is reportedly extremely accurate. The barrel has a 2,000-round life, equivalent to only 80 seconds of fire at the usual 1,500 rpm. (The gun can fire at up to 1,800 rpm). The fuselage adjacent to the gun is skinned in titanium to protect against blast and flash.

The fins were increased in size and were moved outboard

Above: The Su-27's extraordinarily large size belies its agility, which compares favourably with any lightweight fighter.

Above: The Su-27's slightly ungainly appearance has earned it the nickname Zhuravlik ('crane') in Soviet service. The lack of an official name is now bemoaned by some young pilots, who regard with envy Western names like Eagle and Falcon.

Right and above right: Twin braking parachutes are used to give maximum chute area, without scraping the parachute on the runway. Brake chutes are often not used, pilots preferring to use aerodynamic braking and the powerful cooled wheel brakes.

on to the booms which supported the tailplanes. The combined airbrake/main gear doors had caused severe tailplane flutter and were thus replaced by an F-15-style 2.6 m^2 (51 sq ft) spine-mounted airbrake which opened to a maximum angle of about 54°, while the undercarriage itself was refined, with canted-forward main oleos and a completely repositioned forward-retracting nose gear, located much further aft to improve the ground turning circle and to reduce the risk of debris entering the intakes. When lowered, the main oleos are braced at about half their height by an auxiliary arm which projects from the oleo and locks into a socket on the side of the intake duct. This is reportedly to brace the undercarriage for rough field operation. Development of the T-10S was expedited by the continued use of the surviving original T-10s as engine, armament, instrumentation and equipment testbeds, and for pilot training.

The original T-10s had a short, broad, flat beaver tail between their engine nozzles, capped by a dielectric fairing. On the T-10S this was replaced by a much longer cylindrical tail boom which reduced drag and served as a location for the aircraft's twin braking parachutes and 13 APP-50 chaff/flare launchers, each containing three 50-mm chaff cartridges or IR decoy flares. The original tailcone lacked the lateral box-like fairings and the associated RWR antennas fitted to the tailcones of later Su-27s, and contained a much smaller number of chaff/flare dispensers (27).

The first T-10S-1 made its maiden flight in the hands of Vladimir Ilyushin (shortly before his retirement) on 20 April 1981. This was, at last, an aircraft of which Sukhoi could be proud and which fulfilled some of the enormous potential of the original design. Ilyushin himself loved the aircraft, and said: "Before flying the Su-27, I piloted 142 different aircraft types, and always I knew that I was, if you like, more intelligent than the aircraft. Now with the Su-27 it was the other way round. It was more intelligent than me, more capable than the human pilot. Moreover, when I piloted this aircraft for the first time, I knew that this was the aircraft for which I had waited for all of my life. The smile still hasn't vanished from my face on account of the delight I felt in the air, and everyone who flies the Su-27 will feel the same. It's worth being a pilot of this fighter."

Further delays

This first T-10S looked much more like the production Su-27 we know today, although it still had uncropped vertical fins with horizontal tops, and lacked the second canopy frame level with the back of the ejection seat. Extensive trials with a number of aircraft eventually resulted in the adoption of small ventral fins mounted below the booms which carried the tailplanes and vertical fins, these improving both directional stability and spin characteristics. The original 'flat-topped' tailfins were used by a significant number of early production Su-27s, perhaps sufficient to equip one complete regiment.

These aircraft had an extraordinarily high attrition rate, one being lost in a fatal accident which claimed the life of Alexander Komarov. Another had to be written off after losing virtually an entire wing, although the pilot, Nikolai Sadovnikov, actually managed to land the aircraft. Both accidents were caused by an uncommanded pitch-up which ripped off the newly installed leading-edge flaps, causing tailfin damage and loss of the outboard wing panels. One cure was to reduce the area of the leading-edge flaps, and another was to reduce their extension angle. Other problems were less easy to solve.

It is known that the Su-27 suffered major problems with its avionics, although details remain unclear. It is widely believed that at one time about 50 aircraft (often quoted as 'hundreds') were in open storage at Komsomolsk awaiting serviceable radars so that they could be delivered. These problems delayed service deliveries (for trials and evaluation) until 1985, although the first production Su-27 had been rolled out in November 1982.

One of the T-10S prototypes was destined to play a further part in the Su-27 story, providing shocking confirmation that in the field of performance, at least, comfortable assumptions of Western superiority would need to be reconsidered. Under the designation P-42 the aircraft was prepared for a series of world record attempts, challenging the records set by the specially stripped F-15 'Streak Eagle'. The Su-27 was stripped of all armament, radar and operational equipment, and was further lightened by removal of leading-edge flap actuators (which were locked shut), tailfin tips, tailcone, and even the radome, which was replaced by a lighter metal fairing. The aircraft even lost its paint, being stripped back to bare metal and then polished. The wingtips lost their launch rails, and the ventral fins (which may never have been fitted to such an early T-10S) were omitted. Take-off weight was reduced to 14100 kg (31,085 lb), according to figures later provided to the FAI. The engines were similarly modified and redesignated, this time as R-32s. Static thrust was increased to 13598 kg (29,977 lb), an increase of over 1000 kg (2,204 lb) which brought the P-42's thrust to weight ratio to nearly 2:1. The standard brakes could not hold this monster when it was run up for full power checks, so a novel solution was found: the P-42 was anchored to a stationary tracked armoured vehicle using twin cables and an electronic lock.

Flying records

R. G. Martirosov supervised the modifications, which were completed during 1986. Between October 1986 and the end of 1988 the aircraft was used to set a total of 27 records, flown by Victor Pugachev, Nikolai Sadovnikov, Oleg Tsoi and Yevgeni Frolov. These included time-to-height records to 3000, 6000, 9000, 12000, and 15000 m (9,843, 19,585, 29,528, 39,370 and 49,213 ft), a height record of 19335 m (63,435 ft), and time to height records with various payloads. The aircraft set records for Class N (STOL aircraft with a take-off run below 500 m/1,540 ft). The P-42 is still present at Zhukhovsky, and could be restored to flying status if further record attempts become necessary, but a more likely fate is retirement to a museum.

Another early Su-27 (actually T-10S-20) was prepared for

Below: The prototype Su-27UB made its maiden flight on 7 May 1985, as the T-10U-1. Three prototypes were constructed at Komsomolsk, before production began at Irkutsk.

An Su-27UB taxis back past a row of early Su-27 'Flanker-Bs'. The brake chute door is open, indicating that the aircraft has just landed. Almost unique among current Soviet/ Russian two-seaters, the Su-27UB does not require a periscope for the backseater.

Opposite page: Although designed as a PVO interceptor fighter, the Su-27 was also delivered to Frontal Aviation units for use as a long-range air superiority and escort fighter, aimed particularly at the destruction of high-value targets such as tankers and AWACS platforms.

a similar record-breaking programme, which was abandoned for unknown reasons. The aircraft was extensively modified with cropped fin-tips, curved wingtips similar to those of the T-10-1, and with the nose radome replaced by a crudely shaped cone. This, and the extended tailcone, reportedly housed extra fuel. No ventral fins were fitted. The aircraft was intended to beat the world distance record in various classes.

Production powerplant

The definitive production Su-27s (and perhaps the T-10S-1) were powered by the production-standard Lyul'ka (MMZ/Saturn) AL-31F which necessitated a slightly redesigned intake to cope with the greater mass flow, although the differences were not visibly apparent. The T-10S-1 may have introduced the meshed intake FOD protection screens which pop up from the intake floor on start-up and retract after take-off, and may also have introduced the louvred auxiliary intakes below the inlet ducts which provide air during high Alpha flight. The gridded FOD protection screens result in a thrust loss variously described as 400 lb st or 2.25 kN (per engine?) and are actuated by a microswitch on the main gear. The 2-mm square mesh is strong enough to withstand birdstrikes at fairly high speeds.

Above and right: The P-42 was a heavily modified T-10S used to set a series of world time-to-altitude and altitude records, seizing most of these from the similarly modified McDonnell Douglas F-15 'Streak Eagle'. The aircraft was stripped of all operational equipment (and paint) and had its tailfins cropped. For take-off it was tethered to an armoured vehicle by a cable and an electronic lock, allowing the engines to be run up to full power before the stopwatch started.

The FOD protection screens were primarily designed to minimise the chance of foreign object ingestion when taxiing, taking off or landing from rough or semi-prepared strips – an integral part of Soviet combat doctrine even for the PVO. Whereas many Western tactical aircraft need a hard, well-swept runway from which to operate, Su-27s can make pairs take-offs even from stony strips. Such operations are also facilitated by the extremely sturdy undercarriage, which can withstand vertical impacts of up to 6 m/second and which consists of a hydraulically steerable cantilevered single KN-27 nosewheel. This measures 680×260 mm (27×10 in) and incorporates its own separate brake. The single KT-156D mainwheels are larger (1000×350 mm/39×14 in) and their hubs are said to incorporate electric fans for brake cooling.

The AL-31F – a major success

The new engine had its accessories mounted on top, and the new outboard position of the tailfins allowed easier access to these. The AL-31 was designed by A. M. Lyul'ka himself, though it has been improved and refined by the team led by Victor Mikhailovich Chepkin, the present MMZ Saturn OKB Designer General. The engine is a turbofan with a bypass ratio (according to Sukhoi) of 0.59, denoting the ratio of the airflow going through the fan which does not go through the combustion process.

The engine has 23 variable guide vanes in the inlet, and a four-stage low-pressure compressor, with snubbers on the first three stages and a split two-stage stator behind the fourth stage. Its two-dimensional blades are broad chord but of reduced camber and twist. The high-pressure compressor has nine stages, with at least two rows of variable guide vanes. Its blades are of progressively reducing chord and camber. The combustor is annular, and is followed by cooled single-stage high pressure and two-stage low-pressure turbines. The afterburner has multiple radial spray bars and two flameholders and is ignited by sending a hot streak of fuel through the turbine. The variable area afterburner nozzles incorporate inner and outer jet pipes, with cooling bypass air flowing between them to reduce the aircraft's IR signature. Overall pressure ratio is between 23 and 24, meaning that the air entering the intake is reduced to between 1/23 and 1/24 of its original volume. Mass flow is 112 kg (247 lb) per second.

The engine is rated at 12500 kg st (27,550 lb) in afterburner power (when it consumes 1.92 kg of fuel per kg of thrust per hour) and at 7600 kg st (16,755 lb) in military power (when specific fuel consumption drops to 0.75 kg of fuel per kg of thrust). Specific fuel consumption at cruise power is 0.67 kg/kg hour.

The AL-31F has proved to be a major success story, proving as reliable, robust and maintainable as it is powerful. It has a remarkably high TBO (by Soviet standards) of 1,000 hours and a life of 3,000 hours, although every 100 hours the engine is subjected to checks by borescope, oil analysis and vibration monitoring equipment. The 1,000-hour overhaul includes the fitting of a new high-pressure turbine, combustion chamber and some fan- and afterburner-section components with a total value equivalent to 10 per cent of a new engine cost. These and further parts are incorporated at 2,000 hours, with an equivalent value of 15 per cent of new engine cost. Although it is virtually standard in modern Western practice, the engines are noteworthy in being interchangeable left and right and easily accessed for maintenance and replacement.

The engine's most impressive feature is its tolerance to severely disturbed airflow, and its ability to go on running smoothly in such conditions, as demonstrated during tail-slide and Cobra manoeuvres at air show altitudes. This extreme stability is due to excellent intake design and the use of sophisticated computer-controlled variable guide vanes and air data sensors which prevent compressor stalls from occurring. Chepkin and his team are rightly proud of their engine, even in its basic unimproved form, and invite comparison

with the Pratt & Whitney F100-PW-100 or F100-PW-220. They claim higher thrust, better economy in reheat or military power and a longer service life, with a comparable post-turbine temperature (higher than the -100, slightly lower than the -220). The Soviet engine is slightly heavier with 1 cm (0.4 in) less maximum diameter and 5 cm (1.9 in) greater length, with lower pressure and bypass ratios.

An example of the AL-31F has run for 12,000 hours on the test stand, and efforts are being made to further increase thrust, life and reliability. Improved single crystal turbine blades and improvements to the high-pressure turbine heat exchanger should allow higher operating temperatures (and thus higher thrust), although it is interesting to note that the cooling systems are so efficient that the turbine gas temperature limitation is already 100°C (212°F) hotter than the melting point of the blades.

Lightweight airframe

The Su-27's competitive performance is not solely due to Lyul'ka's superb engine, however. The airframe is surprisingly light, considering its strength and sheer size. Although composites are virtually unused, the airframe does incorporate advanced lightweight aluminium-lithium alloys, whose ability to be welded rather than riveted or bolted saves weight and increases internal volume.

The Su-27's fuselage is constructed in three basic sub-sections. The nose is of all-metal semi-monocoque construction, with the stressed skin reinforced by stringers, longerons and bulkhead frames. From front to rear are the radome, the forward fuselage, the cabin and under-cabin, the aft cabin, the avionics bays, the nosewheel well and the LERX. The nosewheel itself is anchored to the rear bulkhead of the forward avionics bay, while the rear bulkhead of the second avionics bay mounts the nosewheel retraction jack and dorsal airbrake.

The mid-fuselage and wing 'centroplane' are basically one unit, with anchor points for the engine nacelles and flanges for the outer wing panels. Much of the structure consists of an enormous integral fuel tank but also has the fuselage spine, mainwheel wells and three-spar wing centre-section.

The wing itself is vast but simple, with full-span leading-edge flaps and inboard trailing-edge flaperons which occupy about two-thirds of each trailing edge. The latter move in unison as flaps to provide extra lift and drag, or differentially as ailerons. Travel is from +35° to −20°. Both surfaces have a single manual setting for take-off and landing, but when under automatic control as manoeuvre flaps have an unlimited number of settings. They are of sandwich construction with a honeycomb core and carbon-fibre skins. The wing, which has about 42° of leading edge sweep and 2.5° anhedral, is built around three spars, with two auxiliary spars supporting the slats and flaperons. The wing ribs are perpendicular to the spars, with extra ribs parallel to the aircraft centreline to further reinforce the wing at the hardpoints. Inboard the wing has massive integral tanks.

The rear fuselage is a less simple and less cohesive structure, built around the central boom which extends back (as the rear fuel tank) to become the tailcone with its brake chute stowage, chaff/flare dispensers and ECM equipment. This is flanked by the semi-monocoque stressed-skin engine nacelles, which are in turn flanked by the two tailbooms, which act as platforms for the tail fins, ventral fins and tailplane, and which contain equipment bays. The slab tailplanes (with deflection limits of +16° to −21°, or ± 10° differentially) have multiple spars and nine ribs, each parallel to the tip. The trailing edges are of honeycomb construction. These operate in unison (controlled by the FBW system) as elevators for pitch control, and differentially as tailerons for roll control. The vertical tailfins themselves are each built around two spars forming a torsion box, with leading and trailing edges of honeycomb sandwich construction. A heat exchanger inlet is located at the base of each tailfin, the port unit being larger than the starboard.

To obtain the desired level of agility (and to reduce drag and weight) it was decided to design the Su-27 to be longitudinally statically unstable, which meant that a computer-controlled flight control system would be necessary to control the aircraft in pitch. This would be the only way of avoiding the loss of control and structural break-up which would inevitably occur if a human pilot attempted to fly the aircraft. The impossibility of flying a modern unstable fighter manually has been compared to trying to steer a bicycle backwards, by its handlebars, while sitting on the bonnet of a speeding car. The aircraft (or bicycle) would immediately begin to deviate from its course, and the deviation would rapidly become too great to rectify. Only a computer can react quickly enough, with sufficiently accurate control surface deflections, to keep the machine flying.

Four years before the T-10 was even launched, Sukhoi had flown the T-4 (Su-100), whose long, narrow fuselage flexed so much that the aircraft could only be controlled by using a fly-by-wire control system. This experience proved invaluable when the time came to design a similar system for the Su-27. This system, designated SDU-27, combines conventional hydro-mechanical controls for the rudders, flaperons and differential taileron movement with a quadruplex fly-by-wire control of symmetrical taileron movement for

Bottom right: Wearing a unit insignia behind its cockpit, this Su-27 is fitted with wingtip ECM pods, a rarely photographed option on all Su-27s and one which is usually seen on aircraft being used in the air-to-ground role.

Below: An Su-27UB lands. The Su-27's enormous spine-mounted dorsal airbrake is shown to advantage. The forward location of the main undercarriage makes tailscrapes a real hazard during a high Alpha landing.

control in pitch. The FBW system also provides stability augmentation in roll and yaw. The system uses four computers, each 'fed' by a separate air data source.

The SDU-27 also performs as a g (+8.5 to −2.5) and α (28°) limiter. These are, however, 'soft' limits, beyond which departure from controlled flight becomes progressively more likely. The pilot can switch off the limiter (or override the limits by using extra stick force to 'pull through' the stick stops) to make brief excursions into the extremes of the envelope. This is how manoeuvres like the Cobra are performed.

Leading-edge root extensions

Designing the Su-27 for instability in pitch allowed the inclusion of the long, flaring wing leading-edge root extensions (LERXes in Western parlance) known in Russia as 'sabres'. These generate lift forward of the centre of gravity (and the normal centre of lift), providing an increased nose-up pitching moment, with this effect becoming more marked at high angles of attack. The extent of this effect is governed by LERX shape, sweep angle, length, span and

***Left:** Pilots compare notes after a formation sortie, a GAZ jeep waiting to convey them to the mess for post-flight refreshment. External ladders are used to gain access to the Su-27's cockpit, rather than using built-in steps, kick-in steps and hand-holds.*

***Left:** A late production Su-27, with no fin leading-edge flutter weights and with box-like fairings on each side of the tailboom. These house chaff/flare dispensers.*

***Below:** A gaudy sharkmouth identifies this aircraft as belonging to a tactical training unit based at Lipetsk. One of this unit's machines has a huge shark painted along the fuselage, fin and nose.*

Electrics
The electrical system is driven by two integral AC generators, each producing 115 V at 400 Hz. They are backed up by a pair of nickel cadmium batteries. DC is supplied at 27 volts.

Two-seat trainers
Many Soviet fighters spawn two-seat trainer variants, most of which lack radar and other operational equipment, and most of which do not appreciably raise the second cockpit. The result is aircraft which are lacking in operational utility and which give the instructor pilot an appalling view forward, normally requiring the addition of a retractable periscope. The Su-27's full operational capability and very stepped cockpits thus marked a major improvement, with the only penalties being tiny reductions in absolute speed, range and radius, with even smaller effects on rate of climb and take-off/landing performance.

Control surfaces
The control system actuates conventional control surfaces, with twin rudders, single-piece slab differential tailerons and single-piece trailing-edge flaperons and leading-edge slats. The latter have only one manual position for take-off and landing, but are infinitely variable when acting as computer-controlled manoeuvre flaps. All control surfaces have hydraulic servos.

Cannon
A single GSh-30-1 30-mm cannon is carried by all basic Su-27 variants, with 149 rounds of ammunition. The two-seater normally has a much larger titanium blast shield surrounding the muzzle, in the starboard wingroot leading edge, although much of it has been overpainted on this aircraft.

LERX
The highly swept wing leading-edge root extensions provide more lift (especially at high Alpha) and further destabilise the aircraft in pitch, increasing agility.

Sukhoi Su-27UB 'Flanker-C'

This Su-27UB 'Flanker-C' of the 234th 'Proskurovskii' Guards Fighter Regiment at Kubinka wears the striking colour scheme of the 'Russian Knights' aerobatic demonstration team. This adds a white forward fuselage and red leading edges to the basic camouflage, with the tailfins decorated with the VVS flag and the undersides variegated from dark blue (aft) to white.

Wing/fuselage blending
The Su-27 was designed around what Sukhoi refers to as an 'integrated airframe' with the wing and forebody blended together to form a single 'lifting body'. This reduces wetted area (and thus drag) while increasing internal volume for fuel and avionics. The F-16 follows a similar approach but makes greater use of composite materials. The Su-27 is of largely aluminium alloy construction, though it uses a great deal of titanium, and advanced aluminium-lithium alloys. The wing has three main spars, with auxiliary spars fore and aft serving as mountings for the slats and flaperons.

IRST
A glazed 'ball' mounted centrally in front of the windscreen accommodates the collimated optics for the electro-optical complex, consisting of a laser rangefinder and an infra-red search and track system. These have ranges of 8 km and 50-70 km (5 miles and 31-43 miles) respectively.

Tailfins
The Su-27UB's tailfins are of increased height, with an extra section added at the base of the rudder. Ram air inlets are located at the bottom of each leading edge, the port inlet being lower and larger.

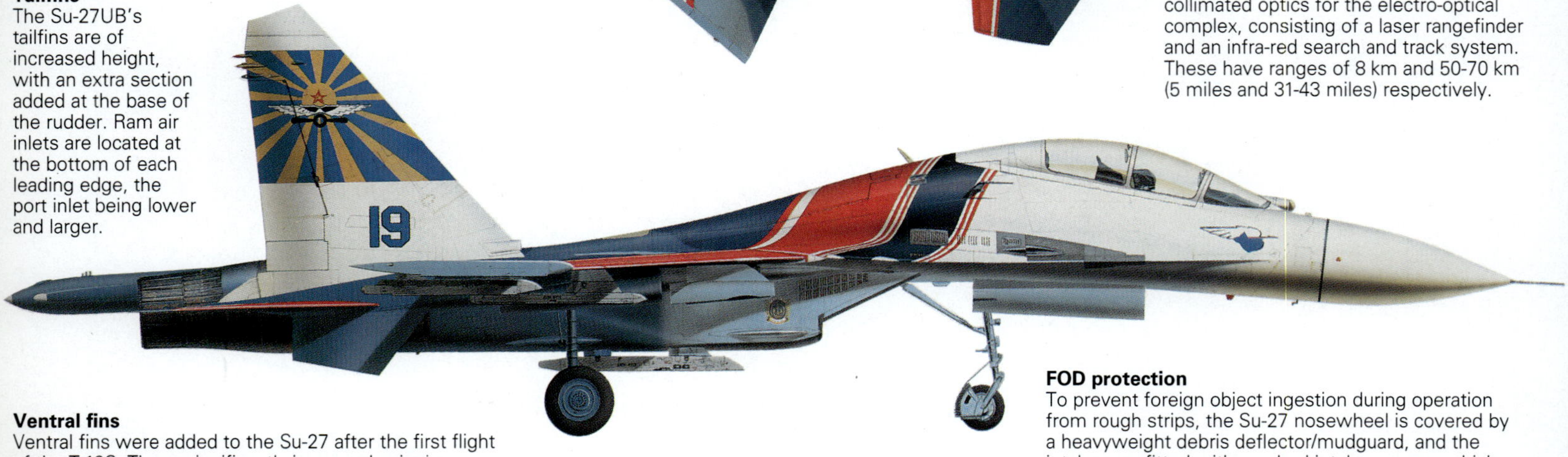

Ventral fins
Ventral fins were added to the Su-27 after the first flight of the T-10S. These significantly improved spinning characteristics.

FOD protection
To prevent foreign object ingestion during operation from rough strips, the Su-27 nosewheel is covered by a heavyweight debris deflector/mudguard, and the intakes are fitted with meshed intake screens which are closed until the nosewheel has lifted on take-off.

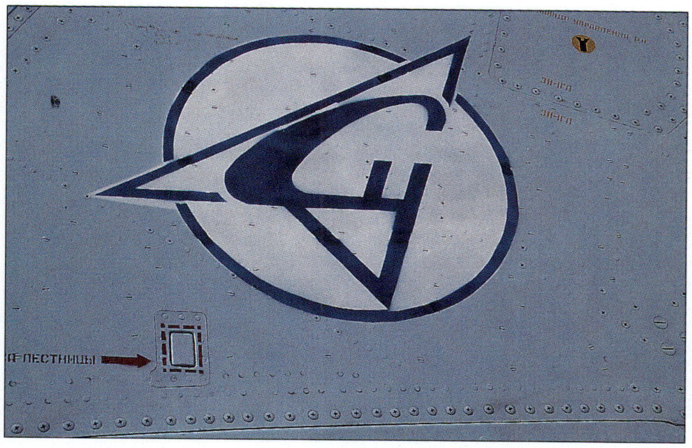

***Right:* The pitot static probe of the Su-27 incorporates wing-like vortex generators where it joins the radome. The radome itself covers an inverse cassegrain antenna for the radar. This retains the same NATO 'Slot Back' reporting name as the MiG-29's radar.**

***Left:* The new Sukhoi OKB logo consists of the Cyrillic letters Su forming an integral part of a dart shape, within a circle. It is carried on bureau demonstrators, and by aircraft of the 'Russian Knights' team. A winged archer was the bureau's previous logo. Factory badges are not normally applied to Su-27s, and few have unit badges either.**

***Right:* The current production standard tailcone accommodates radar warning and ECM antennas in the tips of the square-section fairings along its sides, with a brake chute door in the extreme point. Further forward, flush-fitting chaff/flare dispensers can be fitted.**

***Left:* Prominent ECM antenna fairings (for forward hemisphere coverage) are located on the lower outboard corners of the engine air intakes, except on the Su-27K, Su-35 and Su-27IB.**

***Right:* The taileron actuator is housed in a streamlined fairing in the rear of the tailboom. The differential tailerons are the primary means of controlling the aircraft in roll, and are used in unison for pitch control.**

***Above:* The nose of the Su-27 hinges upwards for access to the avionics bays. This arrangement is quite separate from the radome. The Su-27 is generously provided with access panels, many of them on the underside – a useful feature when the aircraft is being serviced in unfavourable climatic conditions, since the aircraft affords shelter for its groundcrew.**

***Left:* The basic land-based Su-27 has a single nosewheel, with three landing/taxi lights mounted on the forward face of the oleo. The inner surface of the nosewheel door is painted in anti-corrosion Dinitrol paint, which comes in red.**

***Left:* The inner face of an Su-27 single mainwheel. These are fitted with fan-cooled hydraulic disc brakes and are optimised for short field operation.**

Long-range missile armament
The Su-27's primary armament is the Vympel R-27, known to NATO as the AA-10 'Alamo'. This is actually a family of missiles with long- and short-range IR-homing and semi-active radar homing variants, which entered production in 1982 for use on the MiG-29 and Su-27, in place of the R-23 (AA-7 'Apex') and earlier missiles used on previous fighters. The Su-27 carries R-27s on its inboard underwing pylons, on pylons below the engine intake ducts and in tandem between the engine nacelles. The basic semi-active radar homing R-27R ('Alamo-A') is usually carried between the nacelles (as seen here) or underwing, as is the IR-homing R-27T ('Alamo-B'). IR-homing R-27s are seen under the wing of this aircraft. Long-range versions of both SARH- and IR-homing variants have been produced, under the designations R-27RE and R-27TE ('Alamo-C' and '-D') with a boost sustain motor. They can be recognised by their increased body length and a slightly 'fattened' rear fuselage, and on the Su-27 are usually carried under the intakes. Two further variants have yet to enter service: the R-27EM with an improved SARH seeker for use against low-flying and sea-skimming missiles, and the R-27AE with active radar terminal homing, a true AMRAAMski.

Air-to-ground
Although the Sukhoi OKB head, Mikhail Simonov, quoted the same 'not a pound for air-to-ground' dictum used by the F-15's designers, the Su-27 does have a limited and seldom-practised air-to-ground capability. Sorbitsiya ECM pods are usually fitted to the wingtips, and a range of blast, cluster or incendiary bombs or unguided rockets can be carried on the AA-10 hardpoints.

Fire control system
Like the MiG-29, the Su-27 uses three inter-linked sensors for target acquisition and engagement. These are the radar, the NSTs-27 (NSc-27) helmet-mounted target designator and an OEPS-27 electro-optical complex which combines a collimated infra-red search and track sensor and a laser rangefinder. These 'see' through an articulated sensor 'ball' centrally mounted ahead of the windscreen. The IRST has a range of 50-70 km (31-43 miles) and under some conditions allows the Su-27 to detect, identify and engage a target passively, without using radar (thereby avoiding making any emissions which might be detected by the target).

Short-range missile armament
For close-range engagements, the Su-27 can carry up to four Vympel R-73 (NATO AA-11 'Archer') IR-homing dogfight missiles on wingtip and outboard underwing pylons. Developed as a replacement for the R-13M (AA-2 'Atoll'), the R-73 is the first of a new generation of close-range AAMs, with a new level of agility and capable of off-axis launch from all aspects. Some analysts have described the missile as being 'a decade ahead of current Sidewinder missiles' and the 'most sophisticated IR-guided AAM in service'. The missile owes its manoeuvrability to a combination of conventional forward control fins, elevators on the fixed rear fins and deflector vanes in the rocket nozzle. Four AoA sensors are mounted ahead of the forward fins. There are two variants, the RDM-1 (with 30-km/19-mile range) and the RDM-2 (5 kg/11 lb higher weight and 10 km/6.2 miles greater range). Both variants have a 7.4-kg (16-lb) expanding rod warhead and can manoeuvre at up to 12 *g*. They can be fired at targets at 45° or 60° off the nose.

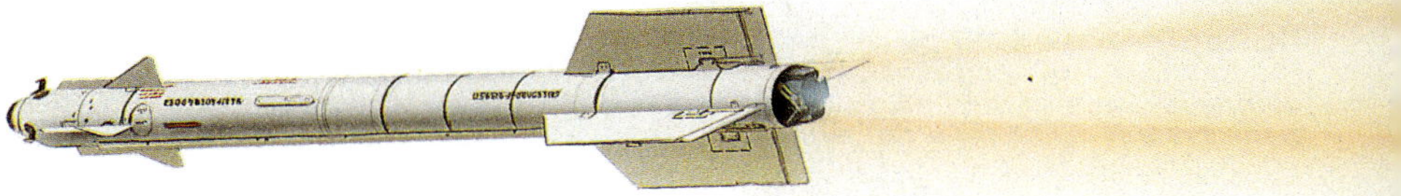

Autopilot
The Su-27 has an SAU-27 autopilot, which is linked to the PNK-27 piloting and navigation complex, the S-27 weapons control system and the SDU-27 flight control system. The system allows the aircraft to be recovered to straight and level flight from any attitude at the touch of a button, and can also allow a ground control station or AWACS-type platform to directly control the aircraft.

Combat persistence
With a typical combat load of six AA-10 'Alamo' medium/long-range missiles, four short-range AA-11 'Archers' and an internal cannon, the Su-27 can engage many targets before having to return to base and refuel. The internal cannon is the same GSh-30-1 as is carried by the MiG-29 'Fulcrum'.

Radar
The Su-27 is equipped with a coherent pulse-Doppler radar (service designation RLPK-27), with an inverse cassegrain antenna. This accounts for the bulged rear section and distinctive double curvature. Detection range is given as 240 km (149 miles), and tracking range as 185 km (115 miles). Some sources suggest that the radar set may be similar to the NO-19 (service designation RP-29) used by the MiG-29, with a larger-diameter antenna, and that it shares the same 'Slot Back' NATO reporting name. Although the radar is powerful, with long range and excellent look-down capability, the lack of processing capacity restricts it to tracking one target at a time. This is of little consequence in traditional Soviet tactics, where interceptors are datalinked to ground stations which provide target prioritisation, but is restrictive in autonomous operations, although all aircraft using SARH missiles like the AIM-7 Sparrow are similarly restricted. The radar display is on a small screen on the upper right-hand part of the panel, but a synthetic radar picture can also be generated in the HUD. Although the USSR obtained much data from Hughes by espionage, the radar is not now thought to be an APG-63/-65 copy in any respect.

Sukhoi Su-27 'Flanker-B'
582nd Fighter Regiment
4th Air Army (Soviet Northern Group of Forces)
Frontal Aviation
Chojna, Poland 1992

Blue 24 was one of the Su-27s allocated to the 582nd Guards Fighter Regiment at Chojna, one of two Poland-based Su-27 units withdrawn to Russia during 1992 as part of the general withdrawal from Europe. Dark green radomes and dielectric panels were applied to early Su-27s, later aircraft having dielectric fairings and radomes in white. This aircraft carries seven red stars under the cockpit, possibly denoting exercise 'kills' or live missile firings. The 'dart and pentagon' device below these is an excellence award, applied to individual aircraft in recognition of their condition as a reward to the crew chief. The excellence award is not, as has often been said, in any way equivalent to American outstanding unit citations. Although designed primarily as an interceptor for the IA-PVO, the Su-27 has also been delivered in significant numbers to Frontal Aviation units. The involvement of the PVO in the abortive coup against President Gorbachev undermined the organisation and led to further transfers of units to the control of the air forces (VVS), which stayed loyal. Frontal Aviation uses the Su-27 primarily as part of a high/low mixed fighter force concept in which the heavyweight, long-range 'Flankers' are targeted against high value enemy aircraft (tankers, AWACS platforms) further behind the front line, but also as a long-range escort for strike and attack aircraft.

***Above:* The basic *IRST* sensor ball used on the standard *Su-27* and *Su-27UB*. This has collimated optics for an infra-red search and track system, and a laser rangefinder.**

***Below:* The inter-nacelle tunnel accommodates tandem pylons for *AA-10 'Alamo'* missiles.**

***Above:* The muzzle of the *GSh-30-1* cannon is surrounded by a titanium blast/heat shield, and is generously provided with vents. The same gun is used by the *MiG-29*.**

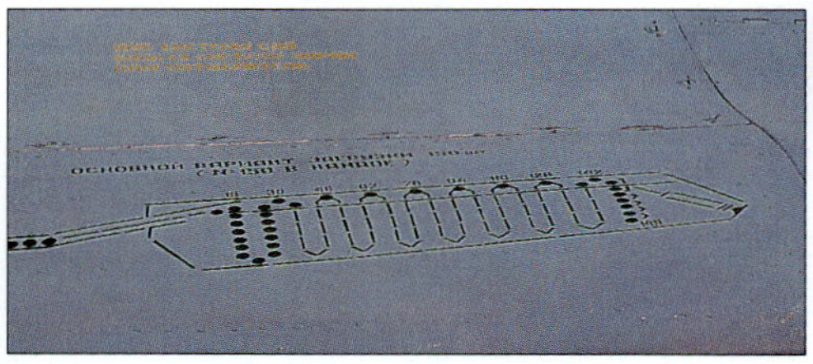

***Above:* A stencil marking on the port *LERX* shows the position and configuration of the 149-round ammunition tank.**

***Above:* The *Su-27* is fitted with enormous gridded intake debris guards, with a fine mesh between the squares of the grid which can be seen here.**

The *Su-27* is powered by a pair of *Lyul'ka AL-31F* turbofans (below). These have distinctive concentric afterburner nozzles (above) with cooling air passing between the two sets of 'petals'. The afterburner spray bars and flameholders are also shown (left).

***Right:** The Su-27's stick-top is almost identical to that of the MiG-29 and incorporates a panic button (for recovery from unusual attitudes), trimmers, squawk, autopilot disengage and missile control buttons.*

***Left:** The cockpit of the Su-27, with an Aresti notation of Yevgeni Frolov's aerobatic display routine clipped to the starboard side of the coaming. By comparison with the MiG-29, which has a very similar cockpit layout, the Su-27 cockpit is more spacious and the pilot sits higher.*

Sukhoi Su-27K 'Sea Flanker'

1 Pitot head
2 Upward-hinging radome
3 Radar scanner
4 Scanner mounting
5 Radome hinge point
6 Infra-red search and tracking scanner
7 Refuelling probe housing
8 Radar equipment module; tilts down for access
9 Lower SRO-2 'Odd-Rods' IFF aerial
10 Incidence transmitter
11 Cockpit front pressure bulkhead
12 Retractable spotlight, port and starboard
13 Cockpit side console panel
14 Slide-mounted throttle levers
15 Flight-refuelling probe, extended
16 Instrument panel shroud
17 Pilot's head-up display
18 Upward-hinging cockpit canopy
19 K-36MD 'zero-zero' ejection seat
20 Canopy hydraulic jack
21 Dynamic pressure probe, port and starboard
22 Cockpit rear pressure bulkhead
23 Temperature probe
24 Nosewheel door
25 Twin nosewheels, forward retracting
26 ASM-MSS long-range ramjet and rocket-powered anti-shipping missile
27 Missile folding fins
28 Nosewheel hydraulic steering jacks
29 Deck approach 'traffic-lights'
30 Leading-edge flush EW aerial
31 Avionics equipment bay
32 Ammunition magazine, 149 rounds
33 HF aerial
34 Starboard fuselage chine-mounted GSH-30-1 30-mm cannon
35 Canard foreplane
36 Starboard wing missile armament
37 Dorsal airbrake
38 Gravity fuel filler cap
39 Centre fuselage fuel tank
40 Forward lateral fuel tanks
41 ASM-MSS missile carrier on fuselage centreline station
42 Variable-area intake ramp doors
43 Ramp hydraulic jack
44 Foreplane hydraulic actuator
45 Port canard foreplane
46 Engine air intake
47 Boundary layer bleed air louvres
48 Segmented ventral suction relief doors
49 Retractable intake FOD screen
50 Mainwheel door
51 Door hydraulic jack
52 Port mainwheel bay
53 Intake trunking
54 Wing panel attachment joints

Defensive systems
The Su-27 is protected by an SPO-15 'Beryoza' passive radar warning receiver system, with antennas on the trailing edges of the tailfins. This gives 360° coverage and classifies, prioritises and displays threats using a built-in threat library, and indicates bearing, range and system-type. It is believed that an active jammer is also installed, though this equipment's designation is unknown. It has been quoted as SO-69 (a transponder designation) or Sirena 3 (which may be an alternative designation for SPO-15). The system is programmed to react automatically using appropriate countermeasures, whether flares or chaff cartridges. The aircraft also has comprehensive IFF equipment with interrogator (possibly SRE-15) and SO-69 transponder.

Engine nacelles
The engine nacelles are anchored beneath the mid fuselage and, together with twin side-mounted tailbooms and a central boom, form the rear fuselage. They are of semi-monocoque stressed-skin construction, reinforced by stringers and bulkhead frames. The whole rear end of each nacelle is of unpainted welded titanium alloy, the high quality welds showing clear signs that sophisticated computer-controlled welding equipment is used in their construction.

Tailcone
The long tailcone projecting aft from between the engine nacelles reduces drag and serves as an invaluable location for the twin braking parachutes and a variety of other equipment items. Perhaps most obviously there are 32 groups of chaff/flare dispensers above the tailcone, each containing three launchers.

Systems
Each engine has a top-mounted gearbox driving various accessories. A hydraulic pump, working at 280 kg/cm^2, is provided for each of the two autonomous closed hydraulic circuits that power the tailerons, flaperons, slats, undercarriage extension and retraction, mainwheel brakes, airbrake, engine intake actuators and anti-FOD intake grids. A pneumatic system provides emergency undercarriage extension, and cockpit and avionics bay pressurisation. The aircraft makes less use of pneumatics than the contemporary MiG-29, whose designers tried to avoid hydraulic systems wherever possible. An On Board Oxygen Generating System (OBOGS) provides oxygen for the pilot, while air bled from the compressor's seventh stage is cooled by air/air and fuel/air radiators and turbo coolers and used for air conditioning and pilot's *g* suit.

Development
The production Su-27 (which bears the OKB designation T-10S) represented a major redesign of the basic prototype/pre-production T-10, with many aerodynamic, structural and systems improvements. Externally the production 'Flanker-B' introduced a new adaptive wing, repositioned tailfins, a recontoured nose and a redesigned undercarriage, airbrake and LERXes. These improvements were prompted by major structural and aerodynamic problems suffered by the original prototypes, which were severe enough to threaten the future of the entire project.

Flight control system
The Su-27 has often been simplistically described as having a fly-by-wire (FBW) flight control system. This is only partially true. The aircraft is statically unstable only in pitch, since this is all that is necessary in order to achieve the benefits of high manoeuvrability, low drag, high lift and reduced weight. The Su-27's SDU-27 electronic and remote control system controls the aircraft in pitch, but provides only stability augmentation to the mechanical lateral and yaw control circuits. The control system consists of four computers, each 'fed' from a separate air data source, with quadruply redundant transducers and signal paths. The system was reportedly based on that fitted to the T-4 (Su-100), which Sukhoi claims as the world's first FBW-controlled aircraft, and which gave the Bureau four years of experience before work began on the T-10. The control system limits the aircraft to +8.5/–2.5 *g* and to 28 units of Alpha but these are 'soft' limits, which can be overridden by the pilot either by switching off the limiter switches or by using extra pressure (about 15 kg) to 'pull through' the stick stops.

Powerplants
The Su-27 is powered by a pair of widely spaced Lyul'ka AL-31F afterburning turbofans. These have a four-stage low-pressure compressor, a nine-stage high-pressure compressor and single-stage cooled high- and low-pressure turbines aft of the annular combustor. Sukhoi gives the thrust ratings as 12800 kg (28,219 lb) with reheat and 7700 kg (16,975 lb) in dry power, with the manufacturer's figures being 12500 kg st (27,557 lb) and 7600 kg st (16,755 lb). The separation of the engines was dictated by the need for a wide inter-nacelle tunnel for low-drag weapons carriage, and to simplify intake duct design, since handling considerations dictated that the intakes themselves should be widely spaced. The wide spacing also ensured that damage to one engine would be unlikely to cause damage to the remaining powerplant, without the need for a heavy armoured titanium keel, as is used in the Su-25 fighter-bomber. The engines themselves are broadly equivalent to the American F100-PW-100 and F100-PW-220, almost the same length and maximum diameter (within 5 and 1 cm/1.9 and 0.4 in respectively) but some 134-212 kg/295-467 lb) heavier. They operate at a similar post-turbine temperature. The Lyul'ka engines are more powerful in both dry and augmented modes, and have a lower specific fuel consumption. This runs counter to expectations, since the AL-31F has a lower bypass ratio (quoted by Sukhoi as 0.59) and a lower compressor ratio, though it does handle a greater mass flow. The engine's most remarkable characteristic is its tolerance to gross intake airflow disturbances (demonstrated by their ability to keep running during a tailslide or Cobra). This stability is contributed to by excellent intake design, and by the computer-controlled variable-inlet guide vanes, which prevent compressor stalls. The very high thrust-to-weight ratio provided by the twin AL-31Fs gives the relatively lightweight and low-drag Su-27 excellent performance characteristics, with an unequalled rate of climb, top speed and supersonic acceleration. It also contributes to the aircraft's excellent sustained turn performance. Victor Chepkin, the engine's designer, has also managed to overcome some of the problems which have traditionally plagued Soviet engines. Engine life stands at a respectable 3,000 hours, and TBO is set at 1,000 hours, although every 100 hours the engines are inspected using borescopes, oil sampling and vibration analysis.

Colour scheme
All operational service Su-27s seen in the West have worn an effective (if unusual) three-tone air superiority blue-grey camouflage scheme. Some reports suggest that a handful of aircraft were delivered in a fighter-bomber scheme of green and brown. Dielectric areas are usually in green or white.

National markings
Despite the break-up of the former Soviet Union, Russian air force aircraft retain the USSR's traditional red star as a national marking, with use of the pre-revolutionary tricolour so far confined to factory demonstrators and civil aircraft. Su-27s operated by other republics have received new national markings.

Sukhoi OKB insignia
Many Su-27s still carry this insignia on their tailfins, and the same badge has also been seen on Su-17s, Su-24s and Su-25s. Variously described as a 'winged helmet' or more correctly as a 'winged archer', the badge is the old Sukhoi OKB logo, since largely replaced by a simple triangle containing the Cyrillic equivalents of the letters 'Su' (Cy).

Tubular fairings on each side of the ejection seat headrest contain telescopic tubes and stabilising drogues.

Right: The rear cockpit of the Su-27UB is similar to the front cockpit, although it has a different head-up display and a system which allows the instructor to simulate emergencies in the front cockpit.

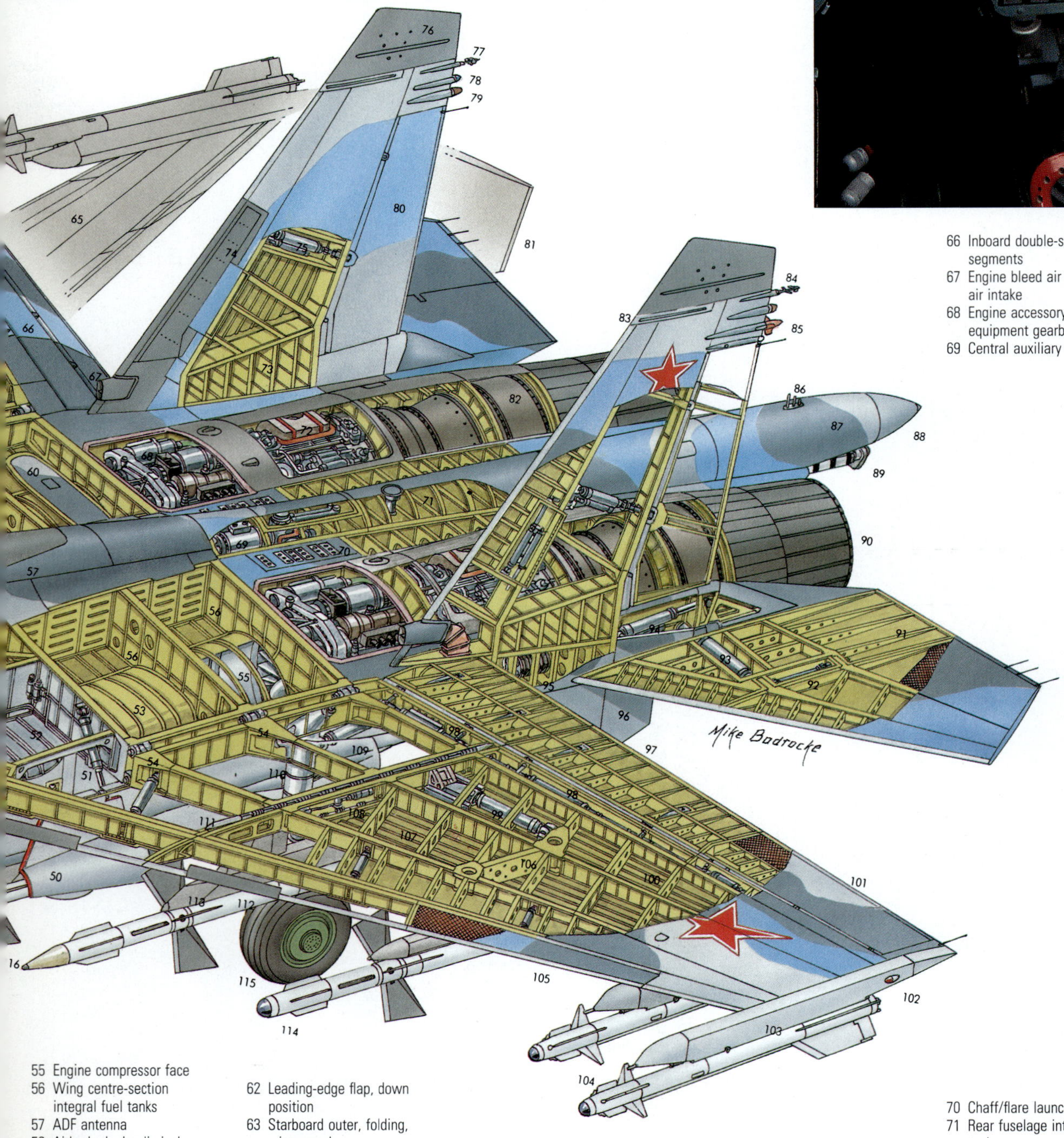

55 Engine compressor face
56 Wing centre-section integral fuel tanks
57 ADF antenna
58 Airbrake hydraulic jack
59 Starboard mainwheel, stowed position
60 Fuel tank access panels
61 Wing-fold hydraulic jack
62 Leading-edge flap, down position
63 Starboard outer, folding, wing panel
64 Outboard plain flap, down position
65 Starboard wing, folded position
66 Inboard double-slotted flap segments
67 Engine bleed air pre-cooler air intake
68 Engine accessory equipment gearbox
69 Central auxiliary power unit
70 Chaff/flare launchers
71 Rear fuselage integral fuel tank
72 Engine oil tank
73 Fin structure
74 Leading-edge HF aerial
75 Rudder hydraulic actuator
76 Fin-tip UHF/VHF aerial
77 ILS aerial
78 Tail navigation light
79 Radar warning antenna
80 Starboard rudder
81 Starboard tailplane folded position
82 AL-31F afterburning turbofan engine
83 Port tailfin
84 ILS aerial
85 ECM antenna
86 Upper SRO-2 'Odd Rods' IFF aerial
87 Tailcone fairing
88 Rear EW antenna fairing
89 Deck arrester hook
90 Variable-area afterburner nozzle
91 Port tailplane
92 Tailplane fold joint rotary actuator
93 Tailplane pivot bearing
94 Hydraulic actuator
95 Hydraulic accumulator
96 Ventral fin
97 Port inboard double-slotted flap segments
98 Flap hydraulic actuators
99 Wing-fold hydraulic jack
100 Outer wing panel structure
101 Outboard plain flap segment
102 Port navigation light
103 Wingtip missile launch rail
104 R-73 'Archer' air-to-air missiles
105 Leading-edge flap
106 Pylon attachment hardpoints
107 Port wing integral fuel tank
108 Wing-fold locking mechanism jack
109 Main undercarriage hydraulic retraction jack
110 Mainwheel leg strut
111 Wing-fold hinge joint
112 Leading-edge flush EW aerial panels
113 Missile pylon
114 R-27 'Alamo-B' IR air-to-air missile
115 Port mainwheel
116 R-27 'Alamo-C' radar air-to-air missile

Below and bottom: The Su-27UB at Paris in 1989 was flown and displayed by Yevgeni Frolov, a self-effacing former aerobatic pilot with no front-line fighter experience who has nevertheless become a vital part of the Sukhoi OKB's demonstration team, and who seems to be chief test pilot Victor Pugachev's heir apparent.

Left and above: When the Su-27 made its Western debut at Le Bourget in 1989, it was flown to devastating effect by Sukhoi's highly experienced chief test pilot, Victor Pugachev, whose dynamic deceleration (the 'Pugachev Cobra') was the highlight of the show. Pugachev was the first Russian pilot to make an arrested landing aboard an aircraft-carrier.

aerofoil section, but is generally most marked with ogival strakes like those of the Su-27.

Any interceptor is only as good as its fire control system and weapons, and although the Su-27 is better equipped than previous PVO fighters, its radar and avionics have been widely dismissed as being inferior to their Western equivalents. The radar is a coherent pulse-Doppler air intercept radar, which may be related to the N-019 used by the MiG-29, with a larger diameter twist cassegrain antenna. It is believed to have the same 'Slot Back' NATO reporting name, indicating (if true) identical operating characteristics and signature (frequencies, PRFs, etc.). Its designation is unknown, although the service designation is RLPK-27. The radar has a claimed detection range of 240 km (149 miles) and a tracking range of 185 km (115 miles).

When the Su-27 first appeared, it was widely claimed that its radar was no more than an unlicensed copy of the Hughes AN/APG-63 of the F-15 Eagle, details of which had been obtained through effective espionage, most notably by a Polish agent. In fact, it now seems that the USSR gained access to the AN/APG-63 and AN/APG-65 when it was too late to be of direct use (although some of their technology may have been incorporated in later Russian radars fitted to the Su-27M/35 and MiG-29M/K). This information was of incalculable value in fine-tuning the Su-27's defensive systems and jamming equipment.

Multiple target capabilities

Experts cite the inability to engage more than one target at a time, and the relatively low number of targets that can even be simultaneously tracked (10), as a major disadvantage. In fact, simultaneous BVR target engagement is limited to those Western aircraft with long-range missiles which do not rely on the launch aircraft illuminating its targets throughout the missile's flight time, e.g. the inertial/active homing AIM-54 Phoenix (carried only by the F-14) and, under some circumstances, in some modes, the AIM-120 AMRAAM.

The lack of multiple target tracking capability is more serious, and is imposed by the aircraft's lack of processing capability (in turn due to Soviet backwardness in computer, and particularly software, technology). More serious still is the radar's inability to keep scanning/tracking while locked on to a target. The Su-27 gets around this by being datalinked to ground stations or AWACS aircraft which keep track of the 'big picture' and assign target priorities. This is not to say that this removes any disadvantage, since reliance on ground stations and AWACS aircraft imposes a level of tactical inflexibility that would be unacceptable in Western air forces. This has also obviously been recognised in the former USSR, where the latest generation of fighters has much better autonomous capability.

The radar is, in any case, backed up by the OEPS-27 electro-optical complex, which combines laser rangefinder (effective tail-on range 8 km/5 miles) and Infra-Red Search and Track System (effective range 50 km/31 miles). These use the same optics, which consist of a periscopic system of mirrors and an articulated glass sensor ball which moves in elevation (10° for scanning, 15° for tracking) and azimuth (60° and 120°) to allow the two sensors to be 'pointed'. The sensor

Above: The Sukhoi OKB's assault on the marketplace continued at the 1990 Farnborough SBAC show, where the Su-27 and Su-27UB gave dazzling displays. Here the single-seater leaps into the air, burners blazing.

Right: The sheer size of the Su-27's dorsal airbrake is evident in this view of the bureau's single-seat demonstrator aircraft.

can be slaved to the pilot's NSTs-27 helmet-mounted target designator, allowing the pilot to cue the laser or IRST on to a target simply by moving his head. The IRST allows the Su-27 pilot to detect and engage a target without using radar, thereby without making emissions which could be detected by the target's RHAW gear.

Medium-range missiles

The primary air-to-air weapon of the Su-27 is the Vympel R-27, a medium/long-range missile available in several variants and collectively bearing the NATO reporting name AA-10 'Alamo'. The R-27 entered production in 1982 specifically for use on the new MiG-29 and Su-27 then drawing close to service entry, in place of (and perhaps even derived from) the R-23 'Apex' used by the MiG-23. The basic semi-active radar homing version is the R-27R ('Alamo-A'), often carried in conjunction with an R-27T ('Alamo-B') IR-homing missile so that pairs of SARH and IR-homing missiles can be 'ripple-fired' for improved kill probability. Long-range versions of both missiles can also be carried by the Su-27, these having a new boost sustain motor and being externally recognisable by their increased body length and a slightly 'fattened' rear fuselage. These are designated R-27RE and R-27TE respectively. Two further variants are under development: the R-27EM with an improved SARH seeker for better performance against low-flying and sea-skimming missiles, and the R-27AE with active radar terminal homing.

A maximum of six 'Alamos' can be augmented by up to four short-range missiles. Theoretically the weapon load could include examples of the R-60 (NATO AA-8 'Aphid') but usually consists of four Vympel R-73 (NATO AA-11 'Archer') IR-homing dogfight missiles. The R-73 was developed as a replacement for the R-60 and the earlier R-13M (AA-2 'Atoll') and is the first of a new generation of close-range AAMs. The R-73 has been described as being 'a decade ahead of current Sidewinder' variants, and as 'the most sophisticated IR-guided AAM in service'. The missile certainly has a new level of agility and is capable of off-axis launch from all aspects. The missile has a very wide-angle sensor which can be slaved to the pilot's helmet-mounted sight, allowing the missile to be 'locked up' at targets up to 60° from the aircraft axis.

Tremendous manoeuvrability (up to 12 *g*) is conferred by the missile's combination of forward-mounted moving canard control fins, 'rudderons' on the fixed tailfins, and deflector vanes in the rocket nozzle. AoA sensors are mounted ahead of the forward control fins. The missile has a 7.4-kg (16-lb) expanding rod warhead. Two versions of the R-73 have been produced, with service designations RDM-1 and RDM-2. The latter missile is some 5 kg (11 lb) heavier and has a 10-km (6.2-mile) increase in range (to 40 km/25 miles).

While its off-axis capability and very high manoeuvrability on launch can be extremely useful, it is not always an advantage, since a hard turn on launch uses up energy and

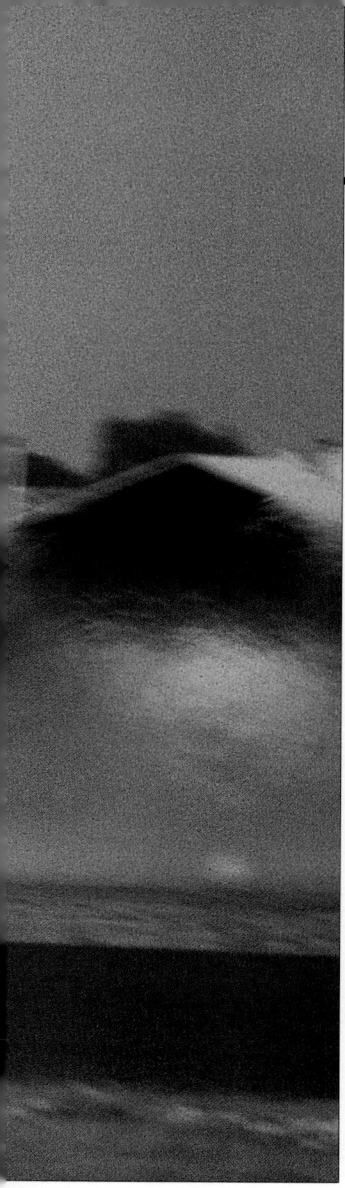

control power very quickly, dramatically reducing the missile's range. Thus it is always preferable to manoeuvre to place the opponent directly in the 12 o'clock position for an IR-homing missile (Fox Two) shot.

With only minor software changes the Su-27 should be compatible with the new Vympel AAM-AE (probable service designation R-77, and perhaps allocated the NATO designation AA-12, though no reporting name is yet known), unofficially dubbed 'AMRAAMski' in the West. This new weapon reportedly entered limited production during 1992, and is primarily intended for the new advanced versions of the Su-27 and MiG-29, including the Su-35, the Su-27K, the MiG-29M and the MiG-29K. The missile has a new monopulse-Doppler active radar-homing seeker developed by the Agat NII, giving true fire-and-forget capability. An improved variant may also have a supplementary IR-homing seeker.

New-generation AAM

The AAM-AE airframe is of similar dimensions to that of the R-27R 'Alamo', though it has very different aerodynamic and control surfaces. There are four very broad-chord cruciform 'wings' (which are actually more like strakes) well back, and moveable control surfaces even further aft, set just forward of the rocket nozzle. These consist of shallow rectangular 'boxes' set at right angles to the missile airframe, with their ends open to allow the airflow through. Set inside these 'boxes' is a latticework of aerodynamic vanes which offer better control at high speeds, high angles of attack and when airflow is disrupted. They also allow small hinge moments, with smaller lower-powered non-hydraulic actuators, saving weight and space. The missile is an excellent close-range weapon, with a manouevring performance of up to 12 *g*, but also has a maximum range of 90 km (56 miles), greater than the short-burn R-27 variants.

The Su-27 carries its missiles on the wingtips (R-73 only),

The Su-27's landing gear retracts forward, the main undercarriage units swivelling through 90° to lie flat in the wingroots.

Vortices stream from the LERXes as the Su-27 makes a hard turn in the moisture-laden English air.

Puffs of smoke from the tyres mark the successful conclusion of another display by Victor Pugachev. The Sukhoi OKB demonstrators hardly ever use brake parachutes.

Above: An Su-27UB leads in two of the 'Russian Knights' single-seaters during the team's first overseas visit – to RAF Scampton, home of the 'Red Arrows'. The team is formed from one squadron of the Kubinka-based 'Proskurovskii' Guards Regiment, which functions primarily as a display and demonstration unit.

The badge of the 'Proskurovskii' Guards Fighter Regiment.

The new Sukhoi OKB logo is also worn by the team's aircraft.

Above: The 'Russian Knights' 'Flankers' carry underwing pylons as a matter of course, and could quickly be returned to operational service.

under the outer wings (R-73 or R-77), underwing (R-27R, R-27T, R-27RE or R-27TE), under the engine nacelle (R-27RE or R-27TE) and in tandem between the nacelles (R-27R and R-27T). The ability to routinely carry a total of 10 AAMs, as a standard warload, is virtually unparalleled, and gives unmatched combat persistence.

In order to use his sensors and weapons to best effect, the fighter pilot must maximise his situational awareness. Achieving this is dependent on a whole range of different factors. To a certain extent, the Su-27 pilot starts out at something of a disadvantage, relying too heavily on outside agencies to process, analyse and present basic target data. Many Western analysts dismiss the old-fashioned analogue cockpit as being a less-than-ideal working environment, and less ergonomically efficient than modern CRT-equipped Western cockpits. Similarly, some Western analysts have criticised the 'switchology' of the Su-27's cockpit, pointing, for example, to the tricky operation and inconvenient location of the short/long-range missile selector on the throttle and the HUD radar cursor on the control column.

The 'Flanker' cockpit

There is a counter-argument to the effect that the familiarity of the Su-27 cockpit (due to strong similarities with the MiG-29, MiG-23, Su-17 and other current/recent Russian/Soviet types) makes interpretation of information presented more a matter of instinct than observation. Interestingly, some Soviet and Russian pilots who have flown both the Su-27 and the MiG-29 operationally also criticise the ergonomic design of the Su-27 cockpit, but are full of praise for the outwardly similar and equally primitive MiG cockpit. In any event, the Su-27 pilot has a very versatile unified head-up display which can present the radar picture and data from the EO complex, as well as the normal piloting, navigation and weapons aiming information presented in Western HUDs.

Cockpit workload is also reduced by provision of the helmet-mounted target designation system. Since this frees the pilot from having to 'boresight' his target, he can maintain a better lookout over the rest of the outside world than if he had to get his enemy directly ahead of him. The system works by using a pair of head position sensors on the panel, on each side of the HUD.

A fighter is about more than just an airframe/powerplant/sensors/weapons combination, however, and the Su-27's 'back-up' systems have been much praised for their simplicity, robustness, maintainability and sensible design. The aircraft has two autonomous closed hydraulic circuits, each operating at a pressure of 280 kg/cm^2, and each driven

Left: 'Russian Knights' Su-27s carry the team name in red in an old-fashioned Cyrillic script on the port forward fuselage, but nothing to starboard. Here one of the single-seaters taxis out at the beginning of a display.

Below: One of the team's Su-27UBs had the front cockpit fitted with rails for an instrument flying training hood. During their visit to Scampton, the 'Russian Knights' flew a number of RAF officers in their Su-27UBs, but few reports have emerged about these flights.

by a separate engine-driven pump. The tailerons, flaperons, leading-edge flaps, undercarriage extension and retraction, mainwheel brakes, airbrake and air intakes and FOD screens are hydraulically actuated. The brake system and control surface servo actuator pressures are significantly reduced.

The electrical system runs using two engine-driven AC generators (producing 115 V at 400 Hz) with emergency DC from two 27-V NiCd 20NKBN-25 batteries. A pneumatic system is used for many systems that, on Western aircraft, would normally be hydraulically actuated. This includes the nosewheel brake, emergency undercarriage extension (a reservoir is located inside the inner face of the nosewheel door), brake chute deployment, canopy opening, as well as cockpit and avionics bay pressurisation. The oxygen system takes air bled from the seventh stage of the compressor for air conditioning and cooling. This is first cooled using air and fuel radiators and turbo coolers.

Production changes

The basic Su-27 has undergone some refinements during production. The current production tailfin shape (with cropped tips and upper trailing edge) was adopted early on, and other changes followed at regular intervals. The most apparent external changes were incorporated on aircraft from the 20th production series, which gained box-like fairings along the sides of the tailcone accommodating RWR antennas and making space for no less than 32 upward-firing APP-50 chaff/flare dispensers, containing 96 chaff cartridges or flares (42 per side fairing, and 12 in the centre). Distinctive anti-flutter weights on the leading edges of the tailfins were also deleted from the 21st production series, and have since been removed from many earlier production Su-27s.

Another modification retrospectively applied to all service Su-27s was the removal of the reticulated polyurethane fire-suppressing foam used to line the fuel tanks. The subject of an embargo, the USSR went to great lengths to import the material for the Su-25 and Su-27, but it proved insufficiently robust and rather troublesome, and has been replaced by a combination of self-sealing tanks and inert gas fuel tank pressurisation. Its only legacy is the number of long access panels in the fuel tanks, originally provided for foam replacement. The fuel used is T-1, TS-1 or RT kerosene, and the average specific density of 0.785 gives a capacity of 12000 litres (2,640 Imp gal) or 9400 kg (20,723 lb).

Radomes and dielectric panels were originally dark green, but have recently been replaced by white equivalents. There may also have been a change in the capacity of the ammunition tank, or to the weight of ammunition carried. Initially, Sukhoi claimed that 200 rounds of ammunition were carried

Left: The pilots of the 'Russian Knights' team, together with General Antoshkin, commander of the Moscow Military District.

Below: The 'Russian Knights' Su-27s wear a colourful paint job, with white noses and red/white/blue leading edge stripes.

Above: An Alaska-based F-15 provides an escort for the OKB Su-27UB demonstrator during the aircraft's first visit to the USA. The similarities between the two aircraft types, in configuration and size, are clearly evident. Another noteworthy feature is the F-15's reliance on external fuel, carried underwing and in conformal 'FAST packs'.

Above: The Su-27s arrive at Oklahoma City, escorting their support aircraft, the massive An-225 Mriya, tailed by a US Navy F-14 Tomcat.

Above right: The first Su-27 to visit the USA was this LII aircraft from Zhukhovsky. It was one of a pair which visited Paine Field in Washington State.

for the gun, but recently the figure of 150 rounds has consistently been given. Stencilled servicing information actually painted on the aircraft gives a slightly different story, with a total of 149 rounds, including 15 housed in the feed to the gun itself.

Avionics systems have changed during the production life of the Su-27, although many details remain sketchy. At least three different IFF systems (SRO-2M, Parol and Marka) have been quoted, while both ARK-19 and ARK-20 ADF/radio compass have been fitted under the dielectric panel immediately behind the airbrake. Current production Su-27s are believed to have an avionics suite which includes A-38 radio altimeter, SDU-10-27 'Command Retransmission System' (datalink), SPO-15 radar warning, and R-800 and R-864 UHF and HF radios.

Changes to the cockpit of the basic Su-27 fighter have been very minor, and the cockpit remains a 1960s/1970s working environment, dominated by conventional analogue instruments. It is well laid out, but intrinsically old fashioned. The pilot continues to sit on a Zvezda K-36DM Series II zero-zero ejection seat. Designed by Bureau Chief Guy Severin, the K-36DM is capable of safe operation at all speeds from zero to 1400 km/h (870 mph) or Mach 2, and at altitudes from ground level to 25000 m (82,020 ft). A version of the K-36 with only minor modifications was even used in the Buran space shuttle. A blast protector raises automatically to protect the pilot at speeds in excess of 800 km/h (497 mph), while the 3.2-kN (719-lb st) rocket (which burns for 0.4 seconds) imposes a peak acceleration of only 20 *g*, minimising the risk of serious spinal injury. The seat employs a KSMU-36 twin-stage ejection mechanism, and incorporates a PSU-36 rescue pack, with a 28-segment 60 m^2 (645 sq ft) parachute. The seat contains an NAZ-8 survival pack with a KOMAR-2M SAR beacon, a PSN-1 inflatable dinghy, food and 'camping tools'.

Two-seat trainer

Although the Su-27's cockpit was such that conversion from other Soviet aircraft (such as the MiG-23 or Su-17) is remarkably easy, the aircraft's unique handling and performance characteristics made it desirable to have a two-seat trainer which would be able to operate over a similar envelope. MiG-29UBs were used by Su-27 regiments as an interim measure while the dedicated two-seat Su-27UB trainer was being developed. The T-10U-1 prototype made its maiden flight on 7 May 1985, in the hands of Nikolai Sadovnikov. Production commenced at the Irkutsk Aviation Industrial Association in 1986, but its existence and the Su-27UB designation of the production two-seater were not

Left: Since the first Su-27 visit to the USA, others have followed on a regular basis. During 1992, an exchange was undertaken between the unit at Lipetsk and the 1st Fighter Wing.

Below: The Su-27 was also displayed at Singapore Aerospace, during which a mixed formation of Su-27s and F/A-18 Hornets was undertaken.

Above: This Su-27 carries an excellence award on the nose, together with a series of small red stars. It was photographed on approach to Chojna, home to the 582nd Fighter Regiment and one of two Polish Su-27 bases. The two-tone radome is noteworthy.

Right: The significance of the 'Batman' logo on the ventral fin of this Chojna-based Su-27 is unknown. Such personal badges (and even official unit insignia) are extremely rare on front-line Russian aircraft, where anonymity often remains the order of the day.

revealed in the West until May 1989, shortly before the Su-27 (accompanied by an Su-27UB) made its air show debut at the Paris Air Salon at Le Bourget.

The Su-27UB, unlike the two-seat trainer version of the MiG-29, was always intended to be fully operationally capable, and was thus fitted with the same avionics suite and weapons system, including radar. The aircraft has a lengthened forward fuselage with tandem cockpits under a single canopy. These are very stepped and consequently no periscope (common in Soviet two-seat trainer variants) is fitted. Sukhoi claims a better view from the rear cockpit of the Su-27UB than is enjoyed by the F-15B/D backseater. While the front seat pilot can see forward over the nose and downwards by -13°30′, the backseater can see forward and down by −8°. The F-15 backseater cannot see downwards at all, obstructions limiting his view forward to +3° above the horizon. The increased keel area forward necessitates an increase in fin height and area, and the area of the dorsal airbrake is also increased. A 740-kg (1,631-lb) increase in normal take-off weight, plus slightly increased drag, reduce maximum speed by about 70 km/h (43 mph) at low level and by 160 km/h (100 mph) at higher altitudes. Low-level range is similarly reduced, by about 100 km (62 miles), and high-level range by 680 km (422 miles). Turn radius, rate of climb and take-off/landing distances are less drastically affected.

Before 1988, little was known about the Su-27. Allied intelligence agencies had seen hundreds of satellite photos and, from January 1987, the type began to be encountered by Norwegian and Swedish interceptors during operations from one or more bases in the Kola Peninsula. Even when an

Right: Chojna-based Su-27s wore very dark blue codes, outlined in white. Most were drawn from earlier production blocks than the aircraft based at Kluczewo.

over-enthusiastic 'Flanker' pilot actually clipped the starboard outer propeller of a Norwegian P-3 with his port fin-tip on 13 September (netting the Norwegians some excellent close-up shots of red 36 in the process) few hard facts emerged. Realisation that the record-breaking P-42 was a 'Flanker' sub-type dawned slowly, and did little more than provide an indication of the aircraft's performance and engine thrust. The Su-27 remained a shadowy aircraft even after the MiG-29 stole the show at the 1988 Farnborough SBAC show, and many analysts expected it to remain in the background, since advanced PVO interceptors have seldom been offered for export (even to the USSR's most loyal allies).

The famous 'Cobra'

It came as something of a surprise, then, when an Su-27 and an Su-27UB flew into Le Bourget as part of the massive Soviet presence at the 1989 Paris Air Salon. The MiG-29's Farnborough performance had already sent a shock wave through the Western aviation industry, and the Su-27 was to cause a similar sensation, shaking more people out of their comfortable complacency about the nature of the Soviet threat. This was almost achieved in a single unforgettable (and still almost unique) manoeuvre, a dynamic deceleration nicknamed 'Pugachev's Cobra'. This was so-named because the aircraft seemed to mimic the motion of a striking snake.

To perform the Cobra, Pugachev rapidly pitched the nose back to an angle of between 110° and 120°, recovering by pitching the nose back to the horizontal. With an entry speed of about 230 kt (425 km/h; 264 mph), and with the power set to 85 per cent rpm, the aircraft decelerated at a rate in excess of 60 kt (110 km/h; 69 mph) per second, slowing to about 80 kt (148 km/h; 92 mph) during the manoeuvre. The aircraft climbed very slightly during the manoeuvre, but height gain is said to be negligible and predictable. There was no tendency to roll off during the manoeuvre and the pilot retained control throughout, being able to stop the pitch-up cleanly and to accurately recover to horizontal flight. The AoA limiter, usually set to 26°, can be turned off, or simply over-ridden by applying an extra 15 kg (33 lb) of stick force. The more forward centre of gravity of the Su-27UB has the effect of limiting the maximum pitch angle achieved during a Cobra to 90°, but the aircraft is capable of performing the manoeuvre.

Manoeuvres like the tailslide and Cobra have a dramatic PR effect, and also have a limited tactical significance. The

***Above:** The stylised aircraft and pentagon badge seen on this aircraft represents an award to the groundcrew, acknowledging the excellent condition of their charge.*

***Left:** Su-27s from both Chojna and Kluczewo stood alert, with fully armed aircraft waiting to be scrambled at a moment's notice.*

***Left:** Later Su-27s, like this Kluczewo-based Su-27UB, have white painted radomes and dielectric panels. Each Su-27 regiment will typically have three or four two-seaters on charge.*

Above: The Su-27s of the 159th Guards 'Novorossiisk' Fighter Regiment drawn up on the flight line at Kluczewo. The unit relocated to Biesowiese in July 1992.

Right: An Su-27 nears completion in the Komsomolsk factory, its markings showing it to be one of the 24 destined for the Chinese People's Liberation Army Air Force.

Below: A pair of Su-27s thunders into the air during the Soviet withdrawal from Poland.

tailslide is an excellent last-ditch method of spoiling an opponent's aiming solution, or of turning the tables in a vertical scissors, as well as demonstrating a remarkable degree of tolerance to airflow disturbances in the engine intakes. The Cobra demonstrates an unparalleled ability to point the nose (and gun, missile seekers, etc.) a long way off axis (away from the direction of flight) and is a phenomenal way of decelerating very quickly. Lost energy can rapidly be regained by using the enormous levels of installed thrust, due partly to the aircraft's low aerodynamic drag. Several Western fighter manufacturers have claimed that the manoeuvres are irrelevant, and that they could be performed by their respective aircraft, although none have so far demonstrated this. The regular inclusion of such manoeuvres in Su-27 air show routines shows a remarkable degree of confidence in the aircraft's handling at the most extreme edges of the envelope, since to perform them at low altitude means that they must be predictable and repeatable.

The Su-27's superb high Alpha capability, which it shares with the MiG-29, is due to several factors, including the FBW control system, sophisticated aileron/rudder interconnects which improve high AoA handling and help prevent departures, and superb aerodynamic design, which keeps air flowing into the engine intakes, keeps enough energised air flowing over the flight control surfaces and prevents the wing from stalling, in the conventionally accepted sense. Wing design is perhaps the key factor, the Su-27 using an adaptive wing with computer-controlled leading-edge flaps (inevitably known as slats) and trailing-edge flaperons. The effectiveness of these is enhanced by the unusual aerofoil section used. The deformed mid-section wing surface is also designed to keep an even distribution of pressure at high angles of attack, which allows airflow to remain undisturbed and

Above: The second prototype Su-27UB acts as a tanker during trials of the first Su-27K.

flowing back across the wing chord at higher Alpha values, and to give high lift (especially during manoeuvring) and low wave drag, particularly at transonic and supersonic speeds.

The Su-27's 1989 Paris appearance has been followed by a number of air show visits, which have won the aircraft many admirers, but few buyers. This is at least partly due to the OKB's inability to aggressively market the aircraft and to distribute information either to the press or potential purchasers. Ironically, the Mikoyan OKB, often regarded as old-school and unreconstructed, has been more open and more successful in this respect than the Sukhoi OKB which has always had a reputation for economic and political liberalism. The 1989 Air Salon at Le Bourget was followed by US air show tours during 1990, 1991 and 1992, by appearances at Farnborough (1990 and 1992), Dubai and Singapore, and by return visits to Paris in 1991 and 1993. Like Mikoyan (which very publicly lost a MiG-29 at Paris in 1989), Sukhoi has had an air show disaster. This occurred on 9 September 1990 during an air show at Salgareda in Italy, when pilot Rimas Stankyavichus failed to recover from a low-level loop.

Foreign pilots

A handful of Westerners have flown the Su-27, often from the front seat. Most of the Western pilots who have flown the aircraft have been senior officers whose front-line flying experience is irrelevant and out-of-date, or inexperienced journalists, and thus there are few independent witnesses who can give a truly objective and useful opinion of the aircraft's handling characteristics (especially in comparison with specific Western fighters) and its likely operational capability. This is in direct contrast to the MiG-29, which has been flown by pilots like John Farley (former BAe Dunsfold chief test pilot) and Bob Wade (6,000+ hour fighter pilot and CF-18 display ace). During such demonstration flights neither design bureau has allowed radar, HUD or other operational systems to be used, further limiting their usefulness. It is believed that the Su-27 underwent a marketing analysis by BAe after the 1992 Farnborough air show, and was flown by BAe and RAE/A&AEE test pilots, but these flights

Left: Still the only known picture of the T-10S-24, the first Su-27 'triplane', is a poor quality image published in the Soviet press.

Below: This aircraft acted as the Su-27K prototype, although it lacked wing folding.

Above: The Su-27K, whose production derivative is to be designated Su-33, is a canard-equipped navalised version of the basic Su-27 and not of the multi-role, glass-cockpit Su-35. It therefore lacks any real air-to-ground or multi-role capability.

Right: The second Su-27K seen during early trials aboard the Tbilisi, later renamed Kuznetsov. Chief test pilot Victor Pugachev flew the first shipborne Su-27K trials.

Right: Before embarking on the Tbilisi the Su-27Ks undertook extensive deck landing practice on the dummy deck at Saki in the Crimea.

remain shrouded in secrecy.

There are good reasons to suppose that the Su-27's formidable handling characteristics do not tell the whole story. During air show performances and demonstration flights, the Su-27s are inevitably very lightly loaded and flown at relatively low speed. At higher speeds and at higher weights, *g* limits, Alpha limits and agility are significantly reduced. Thus the Su-27 pilot's ability to override his various limiters to make brief excursions into the extremes of the envelope is severely limited, and at normal operational weights the Su-27 is no dogfighter. How much this matters is open to argument, since the primary role of any fighter pilot is to destroy his opponent at maximum range from himself and the point he is defending, preferably before he has even been seen. Here the Su-27's supersonic acceleration (which imparts greater energy to a missile at launch), excellent range and endurance and generous load of up to six BVR missiles is much more important than turn performance.

'Not a pound for air-to-ground'

Although designed specifically as an interceptor (unlike the MiG-29, which was always intended to be a more tactical fighter), the Su-27 has been adapted as a ground attack aircraft. Simonov once quoted exactly the same 'not a pound for air-to-ground' adage as was once applied to the F-15, and said that the Su-27 had been designed in just the same uncompromising way. In fact, like the F-15, the Su-27 has always had a secondary air-to-ground capability, although its radar and fire control system lacks software for more than the most basic ground attack mission. MBD-100, -250, and -500 or BD-250 or -500 pylons can carry a range of up to 16 250-kg (551-lb) or eight 500-kg (1,102-lb) blast, fragmentation, incendiary or cluster bombs, or six of the new KMGU cluster bombs. Alternatively, the aircraft can carry up to 80 S-8

Left: As well as folding wings and an arrester hook, the Su-27K introduced a whole new system of trailing-edge control surfaces, with drooping ailerons outboard and twin-section double-slotted trailing-edge flaps inboard.

Above: The cockpit of the carrierborne Su-27K differs in detail only from that of the basic land-based interceptor. There is certainly no provision for any dedicated air-to-ground capability using precision-guided weapons.

80-mm rockets in four B-8M pods, 20 S-13 130-mm rockets in four B-13MT pods (or 16 rockets in four B-13-4 pods), or four S-25 250-mm rockets on individual O-25 launchers. Whereas the MiG-29 has a nuclear strike capability, carrying a single 30-kT RN-40 nuclear bomb on the left inner pylon, the Su-27 is not believed to have any nuclear role. When operated in the ground attack or intercept role the wingtip missile launch rails can be replaced by Sorbtsiya or Smalta ECM pods.

Su-27s have also been used for a variety of experimental tasks and as testbeds for various items of equipment and systems. These have included several inflight refuelling trials, in which Su-27s have acted as receivers and tankers. During 1987 an Su-27UB clocked up a 15-hour 42-minute, 13440-km (8,351-mile) sortie in the hands of Sadovnikov and I. Votintsev. Similarly, the second Su-27UB prototype has been tested as a tanker, with a UPAZ pod on centreline. When the 'Flanker' is fitted with a retractable refuelling probe this is fitted on the port side of the nose, and necessitates relocation of the IRST/EO 'ball' from the centreline to the starboard side of the nose top decking. NIIKAM (The Institute of Aviation and Space Medicine) has used Su-27s to test fly various new-generation cockpits and cockpit displays and even a sidestick

Left: One of the Su-27K prototypes about to 'trap' aboard the Kuznetsov. The new carrier has conventional arrester wires, but has no steam catapult. The Su-27K seems to have won the competition for a new naval fighter, despite being larger and less versatile than its competitor.

The **Su-27K**'s nose oleo incorporates three green amber and red carrier landing lights.

The **Su-27K** displayed at the 1992 Moscow Aeroshow carried an **ASM-MSS** anti-ship missile below the belly, slung between the engine nacelles.

The crude, square-section arrester hook is painted white and black and is carried below the tailcone.

The main undercarriage of the **Su-27K** is modified and strengthened.

The wing of the **Su-27K** folds upwards, outboard of the inboard underwing pylon, for ease of stowage on a crowded hangar deck.

Even the tailplane of the **Su-27K** is designed to fold. Folded, the **Su-27K** is still a significantly larger aircraft than its rival, the **MiG-29K**.

The provision of a retractable inflight-refuelling probe in the port forward fuselage necessitates the relocation of the **IRST** away from the centreline.

control column. Thrust vectoring nozzles (initially circular, but then replaced by flattened nozzles like those fitted to the F-15 S/MTD) have been flown, and the type has served as a test pilot trainer and as a flying laboratory for Sukhoi's ambitious supersonic business jet project, which is heavily based on Su-27 technology and aerodynamics.

One of the most significant Su-27 testbeds was the T-10S-24, which was the result of a programme launched in 1982 to produce an Su-27 with moving canard foreplanes to improve agility and take-off/landing performance, and reduce trim drag. Sukhoi refers to this as an unstable three-plane (canard, wing and tailplane) configuration. After extensive wind tunnel tests, the heavily modified aircraft made its maiden flight in May 1985. The canard helped to offset the reduction in tailplane efficiency at high angles of attack, further destabilised the aircraft in pitch and improved take-off performance by exerting a lifting force on the nose, rather than a down force on the tail.

Export attempts

The basic aircraft has been offered for export to a number of customers, including India, Finland, Iran, Malaysia and even, in a fit of optimism, Australia. One report even suggested that the USA had been offered an option on 20 for aggressor/adversary training. In the early days, when prices were set by Aviaexport and bore no relationship to manufacturing or development costs, Sukhoi claimed that their aircraft's price was no more than 10 per cent higher than that of the MiG-29. Since the Gorbachev revolutions of *perestroika* and *glasnost*, many economic chickens have come home to roost, and the aircraft's price has risen dramatically, both in real terms and by comparison with the smaller and lighter MiG-29 (which is now half the price of a baseline Su-27).

Twenty-four Su-27s have actually been sold to the People's Republic of China. The contract, which stipulated that the aircraft could not be based within a certain distance of the Sino-Soviet border, was signed on 22 March 1991 and the first eight were delivered from August 1991. The aircraft are based on the island of Hainan, and Chinese pilots and ground crews trained at Serov Air Force Academy at Krasnodar. The break-up of the USSR brought a handful of new users, most notably the Ukraine. During mid-August 1992 an Su-27 regiment from Gudauta had to be relocated because of the dispute between Georgia and Abkhasia. An Su-27 was shot down by Georgian forces during March 1993, over Abkhasia.

In Russia itself, the Su-27 was first delivered to PVO regiments for air defence of the Motherland, and then later to Frontal Aviation for tactical air superiority and escort duties. The participation of senior PVO commanders in the abortive coup against Gorbachev is believed to have led to further transfers to Frontal Aviation. The first non-PVO units to receive Su-27s were probably the 582nd Fighter Regiment at

Above: The Su-27IB made its public debut at Minsk, during a closed display for CIS leaders. Laden with advanced weaponry, including precision air-to-ground ordnance, the aircraft was described as a fighter-bomber.

Left: The Su-27IB's boarding ladder is located inside the nosewheel bay, immediately aft of the nose oleo.

Below: The Su-27IB has a broad two-seat side-by-side cockpit for its crew, which is understood to be equipped with advanced CRT displays. The prototype is believed to have been converted from a redundant Su-27UB.

Above: Sukhoi OKB test pilots Ivanov and Ivanov (strangely no relation!) pose in front of the Su-27IB. They are better known as the crew of the Su-24MR that has been demonstrated at some international air shows.

Right: An underside view of the Su-27IB clearly shows the aircraft's new broad, flat nose section. The deletion of the spine-mounted airbrake is obviously less apparent.

Below and right below: One Su-27 (Red 05) used by the LII at Zhukhovsky is used for NIIKAM cockpit experiments, and has a sidestick controller and a single Su-35-style CRT display.

Chojna and the 159th Guards Fighter Regiment at Kluczewo, both part of the 239th Fighter Division at Kluczewo in Poland. Each regiment comprised three front-line squadrons, each with about 12 aircraft (including two or three two-seaters) and 12 operational pilots and four staff pilots (squadron commander, deputy squadron commander, political and navigation officers). A fourth squadron had no aircraft assigned, and had junior pilots undergoing operational training. Until 1990 each regiment maintained a four-aircraft 24-hour QRA commitment, and Su-27s were frequently scrambled to intercept NATO aircraft over the Baltic.

When the new Soviet political order began to take shape, Mikhail Petrovich Simonov was elected by popular vote to the new Congress of People's Deputies, and from there on to the Supreme Soviet, within which he became a key member of the powerful and influential Committee on Defence and State Security, and chairman of the sub-committee responsible for overseeing the 'defence/industrial complex'. From this lofty position, Simonov was able to further the interests of his own OKB, including organising an 'experimental grouping' of R&D, design and manufacturing concerns under the Sukhoi banner, an idea claimed by Mikoyan to be their own.

Mikhail Simonov has naturally continued to energetically and skilfully use his position and influence to further the interests of his bureau, and this has meant that the Su-27 has been less badly affected by defence cuts and drawdowns than have some other projects. Simonov is a mercurial figure, with enormous energy and considerable talent, whose ability to inspire and move others (even in the highly bureaucratic and often obstructionist Russian context) is matched by an enormous talent for design, and for getting the best out of other engineers and designers. He is not, however, a man to

Above: This aircraft, variously described as the Su-27IB or the Su-27KU, made several fleeting appearances at the 1992 Moscow Aeroshow.

Left: This Zhukhovsky-based Su-27 is the aircraft used for cockpit development (sidestick and CRT shown on facing page) and for various other trials.

Right: This unusual device was mounted on the wingtip missile launch rail of the aircraft pictured above. It may be some kind of missile approach warning sensor.

Right: The purpose of this non-standard spine-mounted antenna is unknown, but may be associated with the Su-35 development programme.

suffer fools gladly, and his alleged volatility is blamed by some for his unpopularity in some quarters. He is professionally respected and admired even by his detractors, and the Su-27's success is widely attributed to him, to an extent unknown in the West, where designers are anonymous and aircraft are very much the products of large teams.

Second-generation Su-27s

Simonov's political adeptness has shown itself in many ways, not least in ensuring funding for his pet projects. Because existing aircraft have tended to suffer more funding cuts than new projects, many new Su-27 derivatives have been quickly redesignated to allow them to appear to be entirely new aircraft, and these consequently attract appropriate levels of funding despite being, in fact, merely derivatives of the basic Su-27. Such variants are described briefly below.

The success of the MiG-31 in PVO service has been in part

Above: The 'Test Pilots' aerobatic team operates a handful of stripped-down Su-27Ps and Su-30s as dedicated aerobatic display aircraft, stripped of all operational systems, sponsored by the Jupiter Insurance Company. Here Anatoly Kvotchur taxis in at Boscombe Down's 1992 air show after a gruelling ferry flight.

Right: As the tailslide-performing Mikoyan OKB test pilot, Anatoly Kvotchur was the star of the 1988 Farnborough air show. He returned to Britain as leader of the 'Test Pilots' team in 1992.

due to its ability to operate in co-ordinated groups, covering huge swathes of territory, especially where there are gaps in ground radar cover. As well as freeing the aircraft from the need for tight GCI control this ability has increased tactical flexibility and minimised the impact of limited target tracking and engagement capability. It was therefore only to be expected that the PVO looked very hard at plans to bring similar capabilities to the Su-27, resulting in the development of the Su-27P and Su-27PU (also known as Su-30).

Su-27P

Little is known about the Su-27P, either in terms of its equipment fit or its present status. It is understood to be a dedicated interceptor closely based upon the existing production 'Flanker-B' but with a retractable inflight-refuelling probe and perhaps with the same improvements as the two-seat PU. The Su-27P may merely be optimised for 'group operations' under the control of an Su-27PU. The designation of the Su-27P is not known to have changed.

The Su-27PU is scarcely any better known than the Su-27P, although it has been inaccurately described as a 'command post'. In fact, the Su-27PU is a two-seat interceptor, optimised for long-duration missions, and/or for use in areas with difficult weather/navigation conditions, such as the featureless north, which is poorly served by radar

Right: The Su-27P prepares to take off from Boscombe Down alongside its support aircraft, a Tu-134 used by the LII at Zhukhovsky for transport and liaison duties.

and radio aids. An optional advanced datalink gives a new capacity for group operations, and it can operate as a kind of 'mini-AWACS' with other Su-27s, Su-27Ps or with MiG-29s (for example) as part of a mixed fighter force. The aircraft has been redesignated Su-30, and has been further developed into the Su-30M (Su-30MK for export) with secondary ground attack capability. On a 6 June 1992 proving flight Anatoly Kvochur (a former MiG test pilot now employed at Zhukhovsky) flew to the North Pole and back in 12 hours, with three inflight refuelling 'prods'. The first series production Su-27PUs are said to have been sold to the Jupiter Insurance Company, which uses them (and a handful of Su-27Ps) as the mounts of the 'Test Pilots' team.

Navalised newcomer

The conception of a new generation of carriers for the Soviet navy led to the development of a new 'Flanker' variant, the Su-27K. This was originally little more than a hooked Su-27 with folding wings, some additional corrosion protection, canard foreplanes, a refuelling probe and an optical carrier landing system, although a structural redesign was claimed. Twin nosewheels and a strengthened undercarriage were also provided, to meet the sink-rate requirements of landing on a pitching deck. It was originally intended purely as a fleet defence interceptor and had no multi-role capability. At least six prototypes have been converted, the first T-10K-1 (originally T-10S-37?) making its maiden flight on 17 August 1987. This aircraft lacked wing and tailplane folding, but was extensively used for development work using the dummy deck and ski jump at Saki in the Crimea, where at least one Su-27K prototype has been lost.

The T-10S-37 also retained the inboard flaperons of the basic, land-based Su-27 interceptor, which precluded its use in actual carrier trials. Subsequent Su-27K prototypes have completely new, full-span, three-section, trailing-edge flaps, the two double-slotted inboard sections operating symmetrically as flaps for take-off and landing, and the outboard sections operating differentially as (drooping) ailerons to provide roll control. Instead of the two inboard sections operating differentially as flaperons in normal flight, as on the basic Su-27, the Su-27K is controlled in roll by differential movement of the outboard and middle flap sections, augmented as before by differential tailplane movement. The wing planform and section are believed to remain unchanged.

Another airframe change to the Su-27K is that the tailcone is of reduced length, to avoid the danger of a tailscrape during a high AoA landing. This reduces the space available for defensive systems, avionics and fuel, and may impose a slight transonic drag penalty. This has also necessitated a reduction in the number of upward-firing chaff/flare dispensers carried (12 three-shot dispensers) and their relocation further forward, inboard of the engine nacelles. The Su-27K is the only Su-27 variant so far to be compatible with the carriage of external fuel tanks, in this case a 1500-litre (330-Imp gal) centreline tank. There have been suggestions that at least some of the Su-27K prototypes have been re-engined, probably with the same increased thrust AL-31M that powers the Su-27M/Su-35.

Further tests followed on board the *Tbilisi* (now the *Kuznetsov*) and included Russia's first conventional carrier landing, which was made by Victor Pugachev on 1 November 1989. These tests showed that the Su-27K could take off from

Above: One of two Sukhoi Su-30s operated by the 'Test Pilots' team. These aircraft were the first production Su-30s and were built to a special order with no military systems. They thus bear little resemblance to the full-standard production Su-30.

Below: 'Test Pilots' Su-30s make a flyby. In operational service the Su-30 will be a dedicated long-range, long-endurance interceptor.

Right: The Soviets made extensive use of scale models (launched by rocket or air-dropped) for tests in the extreme corners of the envelope, before risking a full-size aircraft. This model, displayed on its launcher at Zhukhovsky during the 1992 Mosaeroshow, was used in the Su-35 programme.

Exciting air show routines not withstanding, the Su-27 has always been handicapped in service by its lack of agility at operational weights, and by its lack of multi-role capability. This has prevented it from completely eclipsing the smaller, and in some respects inferior, MiG-29 in VVS service, and especially in the export market. Development of an Su-27 with improved dogfighting characteristics and better air-to-ground capability was therefore accorded a high priority, with the aim of producing an Su-27 variant on which the Soviet (and later Russian) air forces could standardise (at the expense of the MiG-29), and which would appeal to foreign operators seeking a multi-role fighter.

Design of such a variant was entrusted to Nikolai Feyedorovich Nikitin, one of Mr Simonov's most talented and dynamic deputies. Under his direction the new variant, initially dubbed Su-27M, received the same canard foreplanes as the T-10S-24 and this 'unstable integrated three-plane' configuration was further destabilised through the clever use of fuel management (including the provision of

Above: The Su-35 (then still known as the Su-27M) was first shown at the closed air show at Minsk. The aircraft shown there lacked many of the Su-35's aerodynamic and airframe improvements, including the tall, square-topped tailfins.

the ski-ramp after a take-off run of 100 m (328 ft) (180 m/590 ft if fully laden), exiting the ramp at 14° Alpha and about 80 kt (148 km/h; 92 mph), in a semi-ballistic trajectory. The aircraft first runs up to full power against mechanical retractable restrainers set into the deck.

The breakup of the USSR led to the cancellation of one of the four new carriers, the scrapping of another on the slipway, and the freezing of the completion of another due to a dispute between Ukraine and Russia over ownership. With only one conventional carrier likely to enter service, the original plan of fielding an air wing with two aircraft types is becoming progressively less supportable, and the Su-27K may be developed into a multi-role aircraft more like its intended shipmate, and now rival – Mikoyan's MiG-29K. The new designation Su-33 is now being used. The existing Su-27K prototypes have already been seen carrying air-to-surface weapons with which they are at present totally incompatible. These have included the new ASM-MSS Moskito, an air-launched version of the Mach-3, 90-km range 3M-80 (NATO SS-N-22 'Sunburn') anti-ship missile. Sukhoi is talking of fitting vectoring nozzles to these aircraft if they win an order. Reports that the Su-33 is based on the Su27M/-35 have been categorically denied by Sukhoi, and it seems that the aircraft is basically a navalised, canard-equipped Su-27, with little multi-role capabilty, and with original control system.

Right: The Su-35 and Su-27 land at Farnborough. The aircraft which visited Farnborough was fitted with distinctive wingtip ECM pods, though it is understood that these can quickly be replaced by missile launch rails.

fuel tanks in the tailfins). The higher level of instability demanded changes to the flight control system, which was replaced by a completely new digital quadruplex fly-by-wire system with four longitudinal and three transverse channels. Extra thrust was provided by the new 13300-kg st (29,320-lb) AL-31SM engine, compensating for the aircraft's slightly increased weight. Vectoring engine exhaust nozzles have been tested on at least one Su-27UB, and are offered as an option on the new variant, by retrofit if necessary. These have a 15° ± vector angle and would improve both take-off and landing performance, and manoeuvrability, but their increased price may not be acceptable to the cash-strapped Russian air forces.

'Flanker' goes forward

The new variant has also been structurally redesigned, with increased use of both composite materials and aluminium-lithium alloys, reducing basic airframe weight and increasing the volume available for both fuel and avionics equipment. The tailfin fuel tanks are housed in a redesigned tailfin of greater height and with a square tip. The lower part of the fin is similar to that of the Su-27UB, but the rudder extends lower and is thus of greater area.

The Su-27M was given a completely new weapons system, with a new N-011 multi-mode radar and a new electro-optical complex, the latter with greater range, angular coverage and discrimination, and with collimated laser and TV designators. The radar may be related to the N-010 of the MiG-29M and is compatible with the use of various new air-to-air and air-to-ground weapons, and has new ground mapping and air-to-ground attack modes. The new radar has increased range, able to detect air-to-air targets out to 400 km (225 miles). Up to 15 targets can be simultaneously tracked (eight while in scanning mode) and six can be simultaneously engaged. The tailcone of the Su-27M has been redesigned and no longer accommodates a braking parachute. It is tipped, instead, by a dielectric radome, perhaps explaining rumours of a rearward-facing radar, 360° radar coverage and over-the-shoulder radar-guided missile capability.

The aircraft also has a redesigned cockpit, with three colour CRT multi-function display screens and a fourth navigation display. These are surrounded by conventional input buttons; there are no throttle and stick-mounted

Left: Moving canard foreplanes increase agility by longitudinally destabilising the aircraft, and by providing an aerodynamic control surface ahead of the centre of lift and centre of gravity. The same canards are fitted to the Su-27K and Su-27IB.

Left: There have been many oblique hints to the effect that the Su-35 has a 360° target detection capability. Interestingly, the tailcone of the aircraft has been reconfigured. It seems to be tipped by a dielectric fairing and lacks any provision for brake chute stowage, leading to suspicions that a rearward-looking radar may be fitted.

Left: The Su-35 has a retractable inflight-refuelling probe in the port forward fuselage, just below the windscreen. This is partially covered when retracted and is developed from the probe used on the Su-24. Small circular antennas are set into the skin, these serving an unknown purpose.

Left and left below: The Su-35 carries streamlined ECM pods on the wingtips, with white-painted dielectric fairings covering antennas fore and aft. A prominent hollow duct is fitted to the inner face, with an open front end. This may be a ram air inlet for avionics cooling.

Despite its huge size, the Su-27 is a remarkably agile aircraft, especially at low weights. A delightful aerobatic mount, by all accounts, the Su-27 is surprisingly easy to fly, although many Western pilots would find its cockpit rather old-fashioned.

Above: Having spent a small fortune getting the Su-35 to the 1992 Farnborough SBAC show, Sukhoi displayed the machine only statically; the aircraft flew only when it arrived and departed. Any extra agility could not be demonstrated.

Right: In the static display the Su-35 was laden with air-to-surface weapons, including laser- and TV-guided missiles.

Below: Like the Su-27, the Su-35 does not carry external fuel, even for a long ferry flight (e.g. from Farnborough to Moscow).

controllers, unlike the rival MiG-29M. Monochrome displays were chosen because Russian colour CRT technology lags behind that of the West, and their colour screens are difficult to read in conditions of extreme brightness or glare. This is a major drawback, since the lack of colour hinders the clear presentation of complex data.

Some Western analysts have suggested that the entire forward fuselage of the Su-27M droops more than that of the standard Su-27 but, while the aircraft does have a different 'sit' on the ground, there is little evidence of greater droop. The cockpit coaming is lowered, giving the pilot a better view forward despite his more inclined seat.

The first of six prototype Su-27Ms made its maiden flight on 28 June 1988, in the hands of Oleg Tsoi. The variant was first revealed at the closed air show at Minsk on 13 February 1992. By Farnborough's 1992 SBAC show, the type had been redesignated Su-35. The prototype at Minsk lacked square-topped tailfins and wingtip ECM pods, and wore the code '706', perhaps indicating that it was the sixth T-10S-70, whereas the prototype at Farnborough was built to a more advanced standard and wore the code '703', perhaps suggesting that it was the third T-10S-70. Some sources from Sukhoi stated that it was the fifth aircraft to fly and this may mean that '704' and '705' were completed to an interim standard, and flew before it.

Su-27 bomber

The multi-role capability of the Su-27M/Su-35 is impressive, but falls far short of that required for a potential Su-24 'Fencer' replacement, a role which many have suggested could be fulfilled by a dedicated Su-27 derivative. Such an aircraft would ideally be a side-by-side two-seater, with a new attack radar and dedicated night-attack equipment, including FLIR. Such a variant may already be under development by Sukhoi. An Su-27 with a side-by-side two-seat cockpit was photographed on approach to the *Tbilisi* during August 1991. The new cockpit was immediately apparent, as were the long flowing chines which flowed forward from the LERXes to the pitot probe, giving the aircraft a nose shape reminiscent of the SR-71 Blackbird. The aircraft was later revealed by the Sukhoi OKB to be designated Su-27KU, and was said to be a dedicated two-seat trainer for carrier-based Su-27K pilots, with side-by-side seats providing both crew with the same approach picture. This is obviously important when a precise approach angle needs to be maintained in order to successfully and safely engage an arrester wire.

Close examination of the Su-27KU revealed a strengthened undercarriage, like that fitted to the Su-27K, with the

Tailcone
The Su-35 has a reconfigured tailcone with a reshaped tip. This is a dielectric radome rather than the usual brake chute cover, perhaps tying in with oblique brochure references to rear hemisphere radar coverage, and 'over-the-shoulder' BVR missile capability.

Cockpit
The Su-35 has a modern glass cockpit with three multi-function CRT displays. These mark a major improvement over the traditional 'steam-age' analogue cockpit of the basic Su-27 but have traditional input buttons surrounding them, rather than the throttle and stick-mounted controls of those fitted to the MiG-29M.

Radar
The Su-35 has a new multi-mode radar, probably designated N-011, with significant air-to-ground capability. This may be related to the N-010 radar of the MiG-29M, itself a version of the Fazatron 'Zhuk' (Beetle). More importantly, the radar has much improved processing, allowing up to 15 targets to be simultaneously tracked, and six to be engaged at ranges out to 362 km (225 miles).

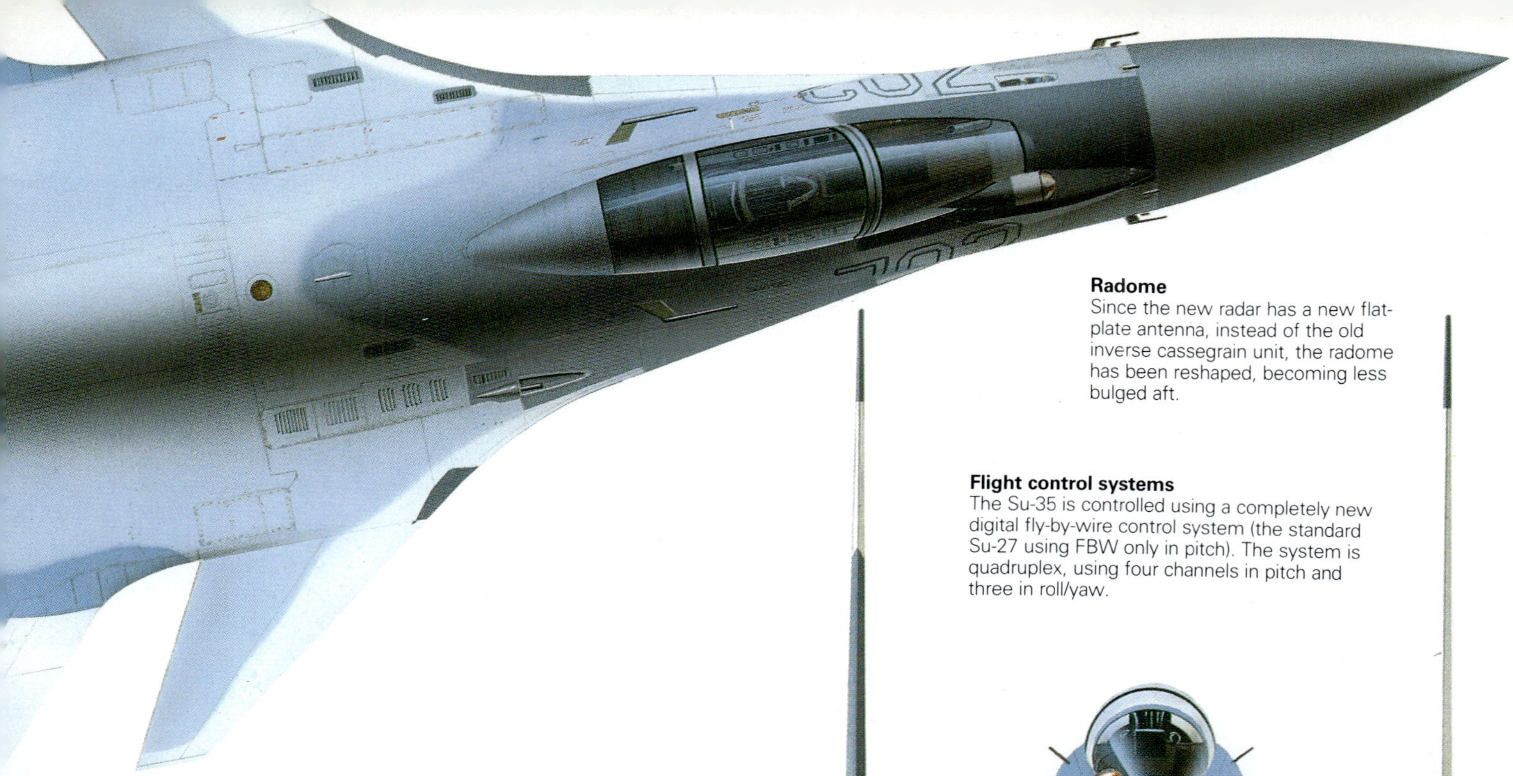

Radome
Since the new radar has a new flat-plate antenna, instead of the old inverse cassegrain unit, the radome has been reshaped, becoming less bulged aft.

Flight control systems
The Su-35 is controlled using a completely new digital fly-by-wire control system (the standard Su-27 using FBW only in pitch). The system is quadruplex, using four channels in pitch and three in roll/yaw.

ECM pods
Wingtip ECM pods replaced missile launch rails on at least two Su-35 prototypes, and are usually illustrated in Sukhoi publicity material relating to the aircraft. The forward radome is reportedly a receiver, while that at the rear is a transmitter, rather than both being transmitters for front and rear hemisphere coverage, according to Sukhoi documents.

Sukhoi Su-35 (Su-27M)

This aircraft is one of six Su-35 prototypes – probably the third, but said to have been the fifth to fly. Both Su-27M/Su-35s seen so far have carried 70 series codes, perhaps indicating the OKB designation T-10S-70. The Su-35 originated as the Su-27M and was designed as a follow-on to the basic Su-27 with better dogfighting characteristics (the primary goal according to its designer, Nikolai Feyodorevich Nikitin) and with better BVR combat and multi-role capability. Although the new type looks externally similar to the standard Su-27, it is in many respects an entirely new aircraft, with many new systems and some new structure.

Weapons
This Su-35 is armed with a pair of R-73s outboard, four R-77s and a trio of the new long-range AAM-L, a very long-range anti-AWACS weapon, whose range can be further extended by the addition of a separate booster.

Fins
The Su-35 has new tailfins (each containing an auxiliary fuel tank), based on the taller fin of the Su-27UB but with the rudder extended downwards to the fin base, as it would be on the single-seat Su-27, and uncropped square tips.

Powerplants
The Su-35 is powered by a pair of NPO Saturn (Lyul'ka) AL-31FM turbofans, each rated at 13300 kg (29,320 lb) with reheat. This is 800 kg (1,764 lb) more thrust than is produced by the standard aircraft's AL-31F, and compensates for the new type's increased weight. The AL-31FM may also have digital engine controls. The engine intakes do not seem to have been altered, so it may be assumed that the extra thrust is the result of higher operating temperatures (perhaps indicating a shorter life, or the use of advanced materials) and not greater mass flow.

Sukhoi Su-27 'Flanker'

Above: The cockpit of the Su-35, unfortunately photographed through the canopy. The prominence of the four multi-function CRT displays is clear.

Right: The Su-35's cockpit displays and HUD shown on a computer screen. Interestingly, the CRTs appear to be multi-coloured, with reds, yellows and greens.

Right: A simulation of the Su-35 cockpit shown at Mosaeroshow '92. Input is via buttons around the CRT display screens, unlike the HOTAS controls which are used on the MiG-29M.

Top right (this page): The Su-35 is optimised as an interceptor, but has a significant air-to-ground capability. This aircraft carries AAMs outboard and ASMs inboard, and under the nacelles.

same twin nosewheels but with an even stronger-looking oleo and with no approach 'traffic lights'. The nosewheel unit has also been moved forward, and now retracts aft to lie in a bay covered by no less than four separate doors. The cockpits were located well forward, with a substantial hump behind, presumably housing fuel and/or avionics equipment. The dorsal airbrake seems to have been omitted, as have the ventral fins. Although at first glance the cockpit canopy appears similar to that fitted to the Su-24 'Fencer', the overhead panels do not seem to be openable, and cockpit access is via the nosewheel bay and a detachable ladder. The two-piece windscreen is very sharply swept.

The credibility of the 'carrier trainer' explanation was somewhat dented by the fact that it lacked wing folding, arrester hook and the redesigned flaps and ailerons of the Su-27K. It appeared to be further undermined when the same aircraft (reportedly one of two prototypes) was exhibited at Minsk in February 1992, festooned with air-to-ground ordnance and with an information board describing it as the Su-27IB (IB being the initials traditionally used to denote a fighter-bomber).

Trainer or fighter-bomber?

Despite this, the aircraft does not immediately seem entirely suited to the fighter-bomber role. The broad, flat metal nose would make the installation of an attack and/or terrain-following radar difficult, and the aircraft also seems to lack

any electro-optical sensors, designators or sighting aids. Furthermore, OKB head Mikhail Simonov has been quoted as stating that the aircraft is "better for instruction in carrier landing and air-to-surface weapons delivery" than as a dedicated operational strike aircraft, and the Su-27IB designation was denied until June 1993.

Thus the Su-27KU (or Su-27IB) remains an enigma. Is it the prototype of a carrier-based trainer (despite its lack of any navalised equipment) or the aerodynamic prototype of a new strike aircraft (despite its lack of attack radar, EO sensors, etc.)? Has the Su-27KU designation been used to cover the aircraft's true purpose? Whatever the answers, the Su-27 is clearly continuing to form the basis of new variants designed to fill new roles, and seems increasingly likely to form the backbone of the Russian air forces as they enter the new millennium.

Left: The Su-35 marks a major improvement over the original Su-27, and is in many respects a match for even the latest generation of Western superfighters. Moreover, it is ready for full-scale production right now.

Below: Political developments have made the Sukhoi OKB the major beneficiary of developments in Russia and the former CIS. Concentration on a smaller number of aircraft types has led to tough times for rival Mikoyan, but since the Su-27 has been chosen as one of the 'backbone aircraft' for the Russian air forces, Sukhoi's position is rather better.

Sukhoi Su-27 'Flanker' Operators

Russia

Sukhoi Su-27s were originally delivered to the integrated armed forces of the former Soviet Union, specifically to the air defence force (the IA-PVO) and to Frontal Aviation. The failed coup against Mikhail Gorbachev (in which the IA-PVO was implicated) led to some transfers of aircraft from the air defence forces, increasing the relative importance of Frontal Aviation as a 'Flanker' user. When the USSR disintegrated, its successor, the Commonwealth of Indpendent States, failed to keep central control of unified armed forces as newly independent states scrambled to set up their own armed forces. Most Su-27s were based in Russia, and therefore passed to Russian control, which retained the same structure for its own armed forces, with separate air forces and air defence force. All Su-27 production is centred within Russian territory, making the country the most important Su-27 operator. A handful of aircraft based at airfields outside Russia were absorbed by the air forces of various new independent republics, including the Ukraine, Byelorussia and Georgia.

***Right:** Somehow emblematic of the new Russia are the privately sponsored Su-27s and Su-30s of the Zhukhovsky-based 'Test Pilots' aerobatic display team. Revenue-earning overseas display tours are the* raison d'être *of these examples of Russia's foremost fighter.*

IA-PVO

The PVO is split into three commands: one controls radar stations, one controls air defence missiles, and the last, the IA-PVO, controls the massive force of manned interceptors. The Su-27 was originally designed to meet the specific requirements of the IA-PVO, with long range, extended endurance, good combat persistence and the ability to act independently or under the control of AWACS platforms or GCI stations. It entered service as a replacement for obsolescent Su-15 'Flagons', Tu-128 'Fiddlers' and Yak-28 'Firebars', as a counter to the new generation of Western low-level attack aircraft and cruise-missile-carrying bombers. The 'Flanker's' look-down/shoot-down capabilities gave the IA-PVO a welcome boost in capability, although production of the aircraft has been sufficiently small that large numbers of less effective interceptors (primarily MiG-23s, but also including Su-15s) have had to remain in service. PVO Su-27s wear no special markings which might differentiate them from VVS aircraft.

***Above:** An early Su-27 on tow at the end of the flying day. At many PVO bases Su-27s are accommodated in individual hardened shelters, but routinely operate from a conventional flight line. Wartime operating procedures would be very different.*

***Left:** An IA-PVO Su-27 in flight. The Su-27's rate of climb, speed, range and enormous warload make it the perfect PVO interceptor, as its creators intended. The aircraft's agility is a useful bonus. Defence of the Motherland remains an important job, even in post-Cold War Russia.*

Frontal Aviation

The Su-27 entered service with Frontal Aviation (part of the VVS or Air Forces) for long-range air superiority and as an escort fighter. It was seen as being particularly useful for the destruction of high-value targets behind the enemy front line, including tankers and AWACS aircraft. Units believed to be Frontal Aviation operators of the Su-27 include: 234th 'Proskurovskii' Guards IAP, including the 'Russian Knights' team at Kubinka (Moscow Military District); 159th 'Novorossiisk' Guards IAP at Kluczewo, Poland, then at Biesowice; 582nd IAP at Chojna, Poland, then flown to Smolensk to disband; 831st IAP at Mirgorod (Carpathian Military District); 54th IAP at Vainodo, and 689th IAP at Nivenskoye (both Leningrad MD); and the 61st IAP at Baranovidu and the 62nd IAP at Bielbek, which respectively became parts of the Byelorussian and Ukrainian air forces. Other Ukrainian-based Su-27 units were at Zhitomir and Sevastapol. An unknown regiment is based at Gaduata, and may be under Georgian control. Some of the units listed may have been (or may still be) under IA-PVO control.

Above: The blue and gold sunburst flag of the VVS is proudly worn on the tailfins of the 'Russian Knights' Su-27s. The IA-PVO is not part of the Russian air forces, which have their own regiments of Su-27s.

Above: For Frontal Aviation the Su-27 is a long-range complement to the MiG-29, specialising in the escort of strike aircraft and the destruction of high-value airborne targets further behind the enemy front line.

Right: The 'Russian Knights' team comes under the direct control of Frontal Aviation, as part of the Kubinka-based 234 'Proskurovskii' Guards IAP (Fighter Regiment).

AV-MF

The naval air arm is not believed to have any significant number of land-based Su-27s, though a handful may have been taken on charge for training duties, pending the service introduction of the carrierborne Su-27K/Su-33. The Su-27 has been selected as the aircraft which will equip the air wing of Russia's only conventional aircraft-carrier, the *Kuznetsov*. Originally there were to have been four such carriers, but one was cancelled, another (*Ulyanovsk*) was broken up on the slipway, and the third, *Varyag*, awaits its electronics, if the ownership dispute between Russia and the Ukraine can ever be solved. With four carriers planned, the USSR expected to field a dedicated long-range interceptor (the Su-27K) and a smaller multi-role fighter-bomber (the MiG-29K). With only one carrier it now seems likely that only one type will be procured, and Sukhoi's political ascendancy makes it almost certain that this will be the Su-27K, despite its lack of multi-role capability and very large size. This will increase cost, and reduce the number of aircraft that can be carried by comparison with an air wing composed entirely of MiG-29Ks. A batch of 20 Su-27Ks is reportedly nearing completion.

Above: Victor Pugachev blasts off from the Tbilisi to make Russia's second carrier take-off, having been preceded by Takhtar Aubakirov in the MiG-29K.

Left: The Su-27K is almost certain to be the only fixed-wing aircraft type deployed aboard the Kuznetsov when it finally becomes operational. It seems likely to be redesignated Su-33.

Experimental establishments

Despite its importance as a front-line fighter, relatively large numbers of Su-27s are in use as testbeds and trials aircraft, mostly at the massive experimental airfield at Zhukhovsky, known as the LII. Some of these aircraft fly missions on behalf of TsAGI (The Central Hydrodynamics Institute), while others are used for avaition medicine, cockpit trials and 'human factors' research by NIIKAM. Additional aircraft are used as engine testbeds, including at least one fitted with a massive two-dimensional thrust-vectoring engine nozzle. The Gromov Flight Research Centre is also home to a test pilots school, which uses Su-27s for training, and as the mount for its commercially sponsored aerobatic display team, led by Anatoly Kvotchur. The team's aircraft are actually Su-30s and Su-27Ps. Su-27s are also used as weapons trials work-horses, hauling aloft both air-to-air and air-to-surface weapons.

Right: The Su-30 (foreground) and Su-27P of the 'Test Pilots' team on approach at Woodford's 1992 air show. The aircraft are frequent visitors to Western air shows.

Sukhoi OKB

The Sukhoi Design Bureau itself uses a number of Su-27s for trials, tests and demonstration work, although the dividing line between Zhukhovsky- and Sukhoi-owned aircraft is a very fine one. It may be that the OKB aircraft are leased back or loaned back to the bureau, but actually belong to the Flight Research Institute. The well-known Paris/Farnborough/US/Singapore pair of aircraft seems to be on permanent OKB charge, but the bureau also appears to have unlimited access to the Su-27IB prototype, several Su-27Ks and a handful of Su-35s. The old P-42 record breaker is in external store at Zhukhovsky, and may be on OKB charge. The OKB does have its own pool of dedicated test pilots, led by Victor Pugachev.

Right: Sukhoi's aircraft are used for displays and customer demonstrations, and have become a well-known feature of the Western air show circuit.

Below: This Su-35 is used by the Sukhoi OKB as a demonstrator. The aircraft carries the old-style winged archer logo on its tailfins.

Right: The Sukhoi OKB's Su-27UB demonstrator lands at Oklahoma City. The bureau has its own Il-76s, but used the An-225 as a support aircraft during the Su-27's US tour.

Independent states

After the break-up of the former USSR, several Su-27 regiments were left on the soil of new republics. Some aircraft were flown back to Russia by their (predominantly Russian) pilots but others were used to form the basis of a number of new independent air arms. The Su-27, as the most capable Soviet-built fighter in service, is obviously a highly sought-after symbol of national power and pride. In the Ukraine, Su-27s serve at Zhitomir, Bielbek and Sevastapol, the former aircraft being decorated with an eagle and sun badge. All Ukrainian aircraft are gradually receiving new national insignia, consisting of a golden stylised trident on a blue disc. This is applied to the tailfins of most Ukrainian aircraft. A blue and gold roundel is carried above and below the wings. The old Soviet red star marking is being removed with haste. At least one Su-27 was offered for sale by the Ukraine, in a mass sell-off of surplus aircraft inherited from former Soviet units based in the Republic. In Byelorussia Su-27s serve with the former 61st IAP at Baranovidu, and it is believed that Georgia may also have its own Su-27s. The national markings worn by these aircraft (if any) remain a matter for conjecture. In all non-Russian states, operation of the Su-27 is dependent upon keeping the supply of spares open, and the supply of trained pilots (many of whom are native Russians) is another complicating factor. These difficulties may well lead to the sale of the Ukrainian Su-27s, and their replacement by types which are easier to support and maintain locally or which are in service in larger numbers.

Right: This badge was applied to the tailfins of Zhitomir-based Su-27s. It has reportedly been retained since the unit came under Ukrainian control.

Below: This Su-27 was photographed in full Ukrainian national markings at an airshow at one of the Antonov OKB's test airfields.

China

The first true export customer for the Su-27 was the People's Republic of China, whose People's Liberation Army Air Force has taken delivery of some 24 Su-27s (sometimes quoted as 22 aircraft). The number of Su-27UB two-seat trainers included in (or additional to) this total remains unknown. The delivery of the Su-27s to China marks the first large weapons purchase from the USSR/Russia since the big split during the 1960s, and gives China its first truly modern fighter aircraft, although the extent to which the Su-27s have been downgraded remains uncertain. Chinese Su-27s were delivered in a new medium grey colour scheme with the red 'star and bar' on the tailfins and on the wings. A two-digit code (ranging up to 24, at least) is applied to the nose, below the windscreen. The contract originally stipulated that the Su-27s could not be based near the Sino-Soviet border, and the aircraft were initially delivered to a base on Hainan Island, facing the Taiwanese threat. More recently there have been reports that China has broken the basing agreement and moved the 'Flankers' to a base near the Russian border.

The last of China's 24 Su-27s is seen outside the Komsomolsk factory. The colour scheme worn by these aircraft includes an unusual 'cut-out' in the lower part of the radome.

Sukhoi Su-27 family

These highly accurate plans are reproduced at 1:72 scale, which gives a ratio of one inch to six feet. This allows a tremendous amount of detail to be shown, and shows distinctive features more clearly than most photographs. The plans were especially commissioned for this book, and are the most accurate ever published. They were prepared using many sources of reference, including Sukhoi-supplied drawings and figures, and measurement of actual aircraft by the artist and editors.

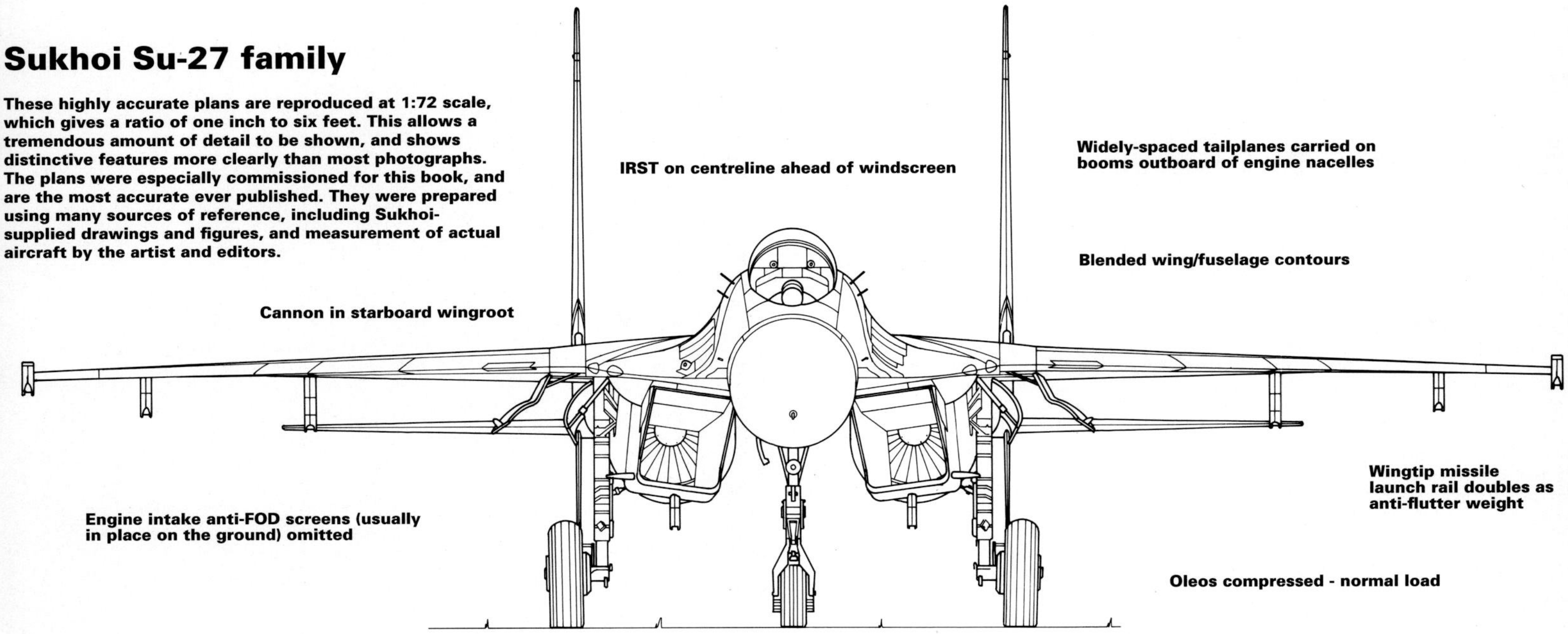

Late production Sukhoi Su-27 (front view)

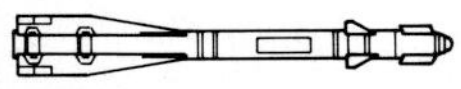

R-60M (US/NATO designation AA-8 'Aphid')

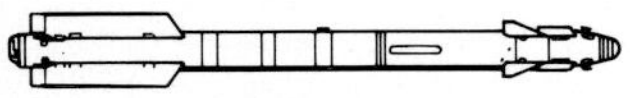

R-73 RMD2 (US/NATO AA-11 'Archer')

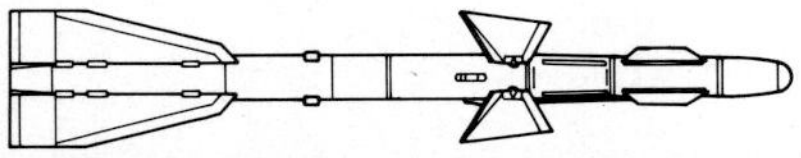

R-27T (US/NATO designation AA-10 'Alamo-B')

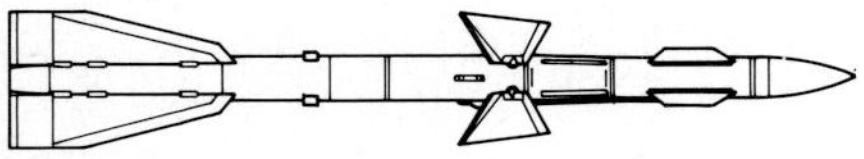

R-27R (US/NATO designation AA-10 'Alamo-A')

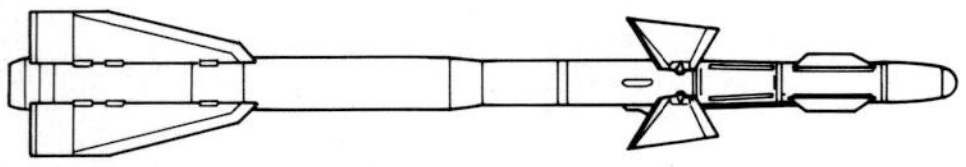

R-27ET (US/NATO designation AA-10 'Alamo-D')

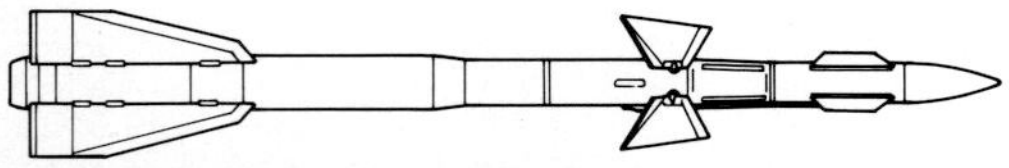

R-27ER/RZ (US/NATO designation AA-10 'Alamo-C')

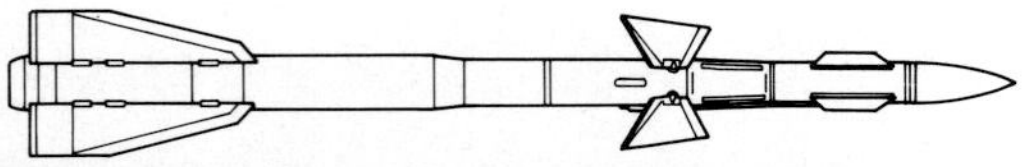

R-27AE/EZ (Active radar version under development)

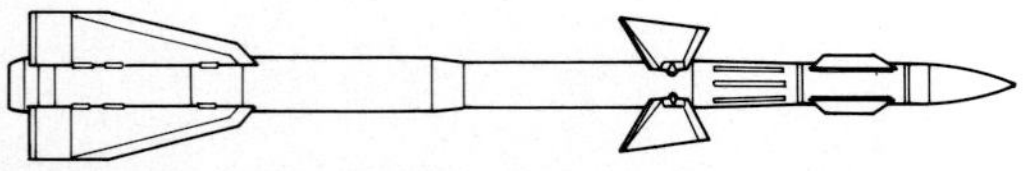

R-27EM (Extended-range version under development)

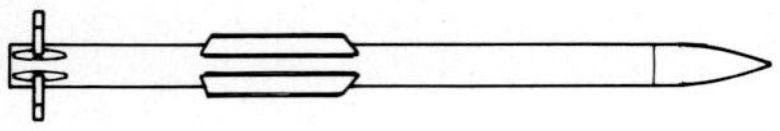

R-77/AAM-AE 'AMRAAMSki' (US designation AA-X-12)

APU outboard pylon for R-27

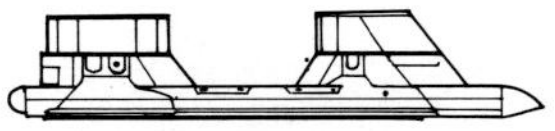

APU-470 inboard underwing pylon for R-27

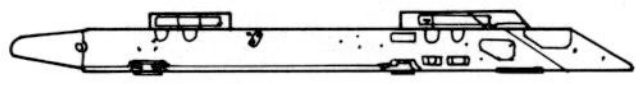

AKU-470 underfuselage and intake pylon for R-27

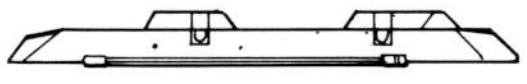

Dedicated Kh-31 pylon

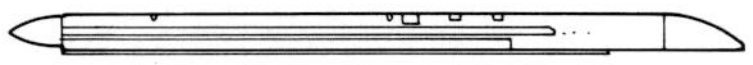

AKU-58 dedicated Kh-58 pylon

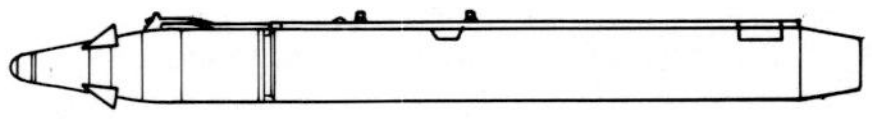

S-25M Su-30M, Su-34 and Su-35 only

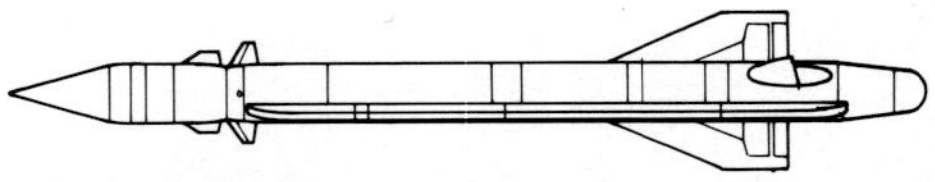

Kh-25MP (US/NATO AS-12 'Kegler') Su-30M, Su-34 and Su-35 only

Su-30M, Su-34 and Su-35 only

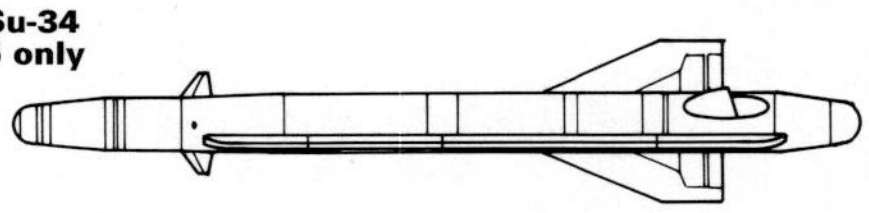

Kh-25MD/ML (US/NATO AS-10 'Karen')

Su-30M, Su-34 and Su-35 only

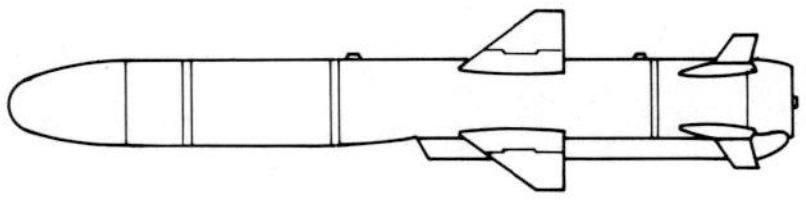

Kh-35 'Harpoonski' (based on SS-N-25)

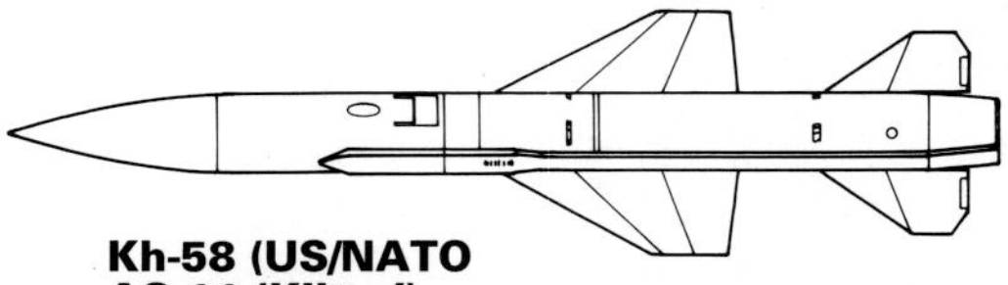

Kh-58 (US/NATO AS-11 'Kilter') Su-30M, Su-34 and Su-35 only

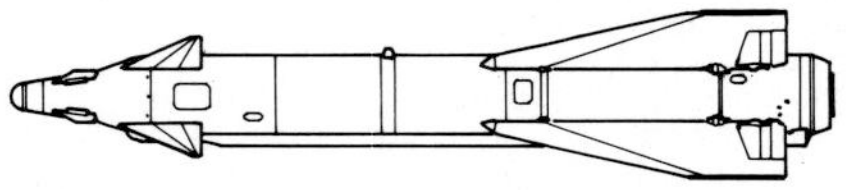

Kh-29L (US/NATO AS-14 'Kedge')

Su-30M, Su-34 and Su-35 only

Su-30M, Su-34 and Su-35 only

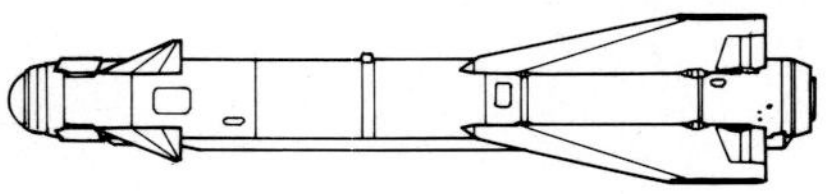

Kh-29T (US/NATO AS-14 'Kedge')

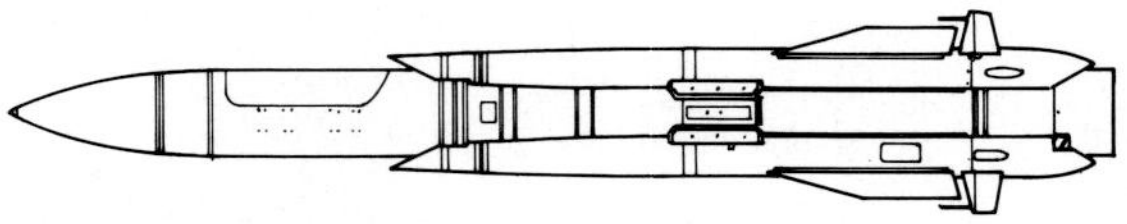

Kh-31P (US/NATO AS-17 'Krypton')

Behind the passive radar homing seeker is the warhead, with the battery, autopilot and powerpack behind that

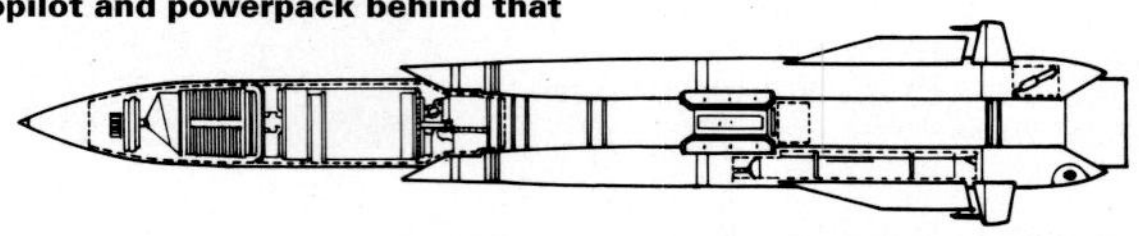

Kh-31 cutaway

The Kh-31 has a booster and ramjet sustainer behind the centre section fuel tank. Control fins are actuated pneumatically

Sukhoi T-10 prototypes

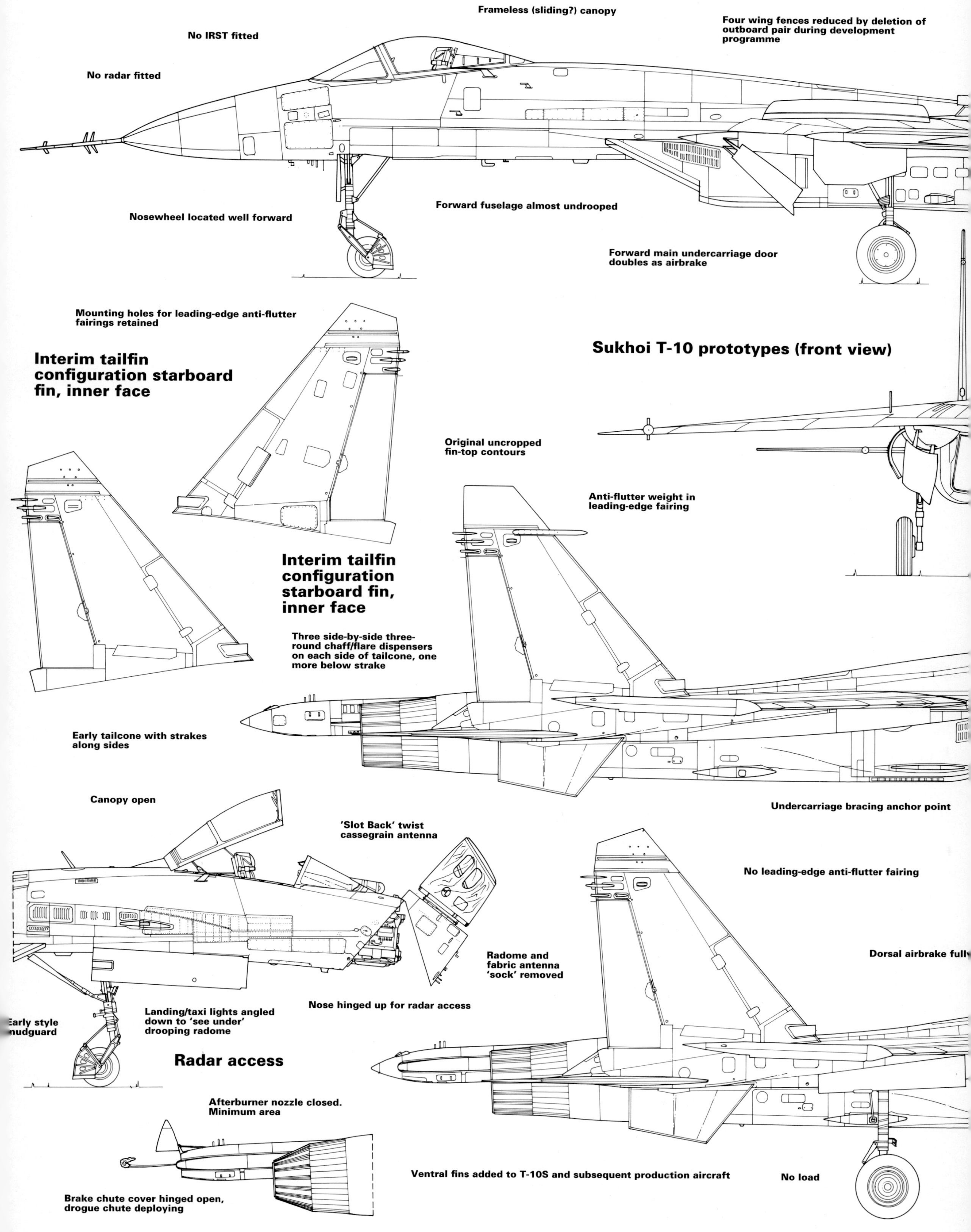

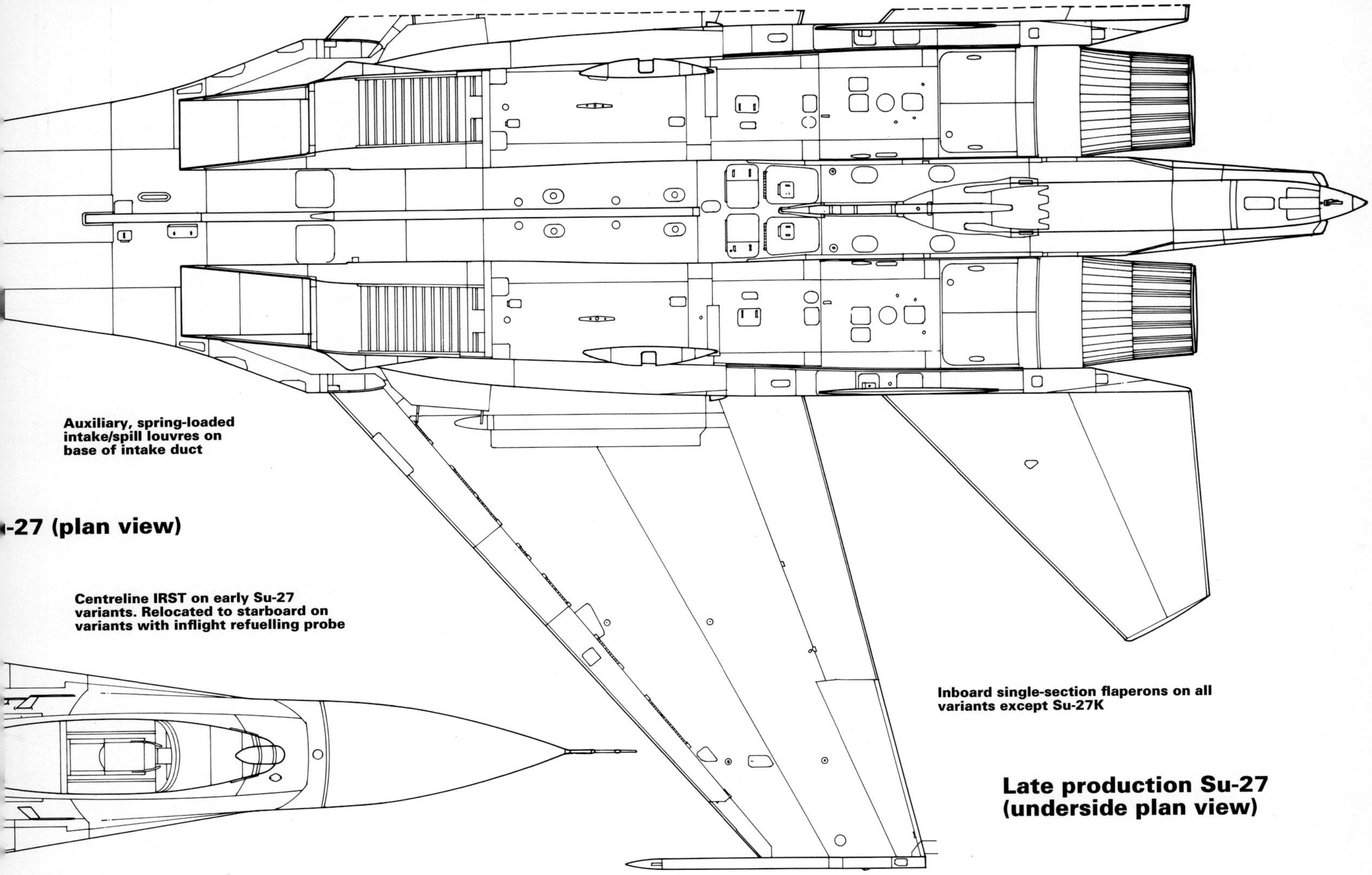

Auxiliary, spring-loaded intake/spill louvres on base of intake duct

-27 (plan view)

Centreline IRST on early Su-27 variants. Relocated to starboard on variants with inflight refuelling probe

Inboard single-section flaperons on all variants except Su-27K

Late production Su-27 (underside plan view)

ction Su-27UB

give
ter excellent view
nose

Production aircraft have short pitot probe

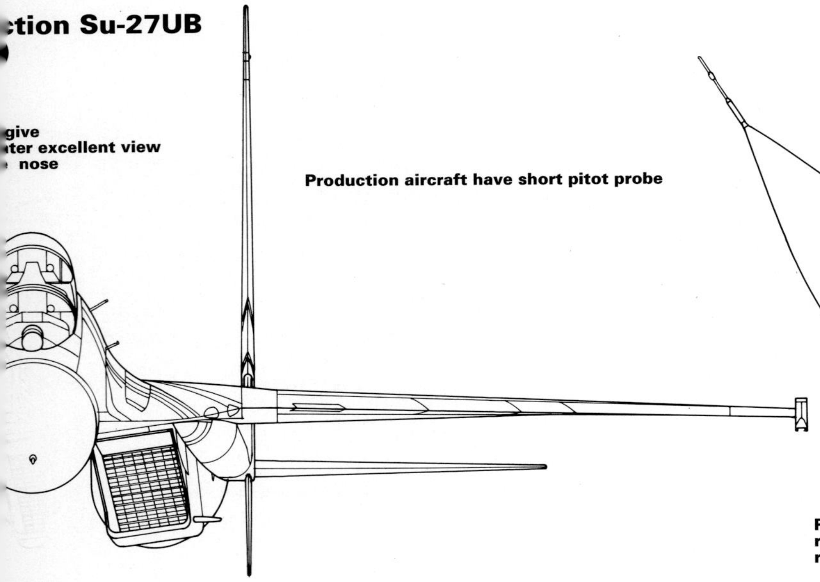

n screens seen in position

Su-27UB (partial side view)

Canopy fully open

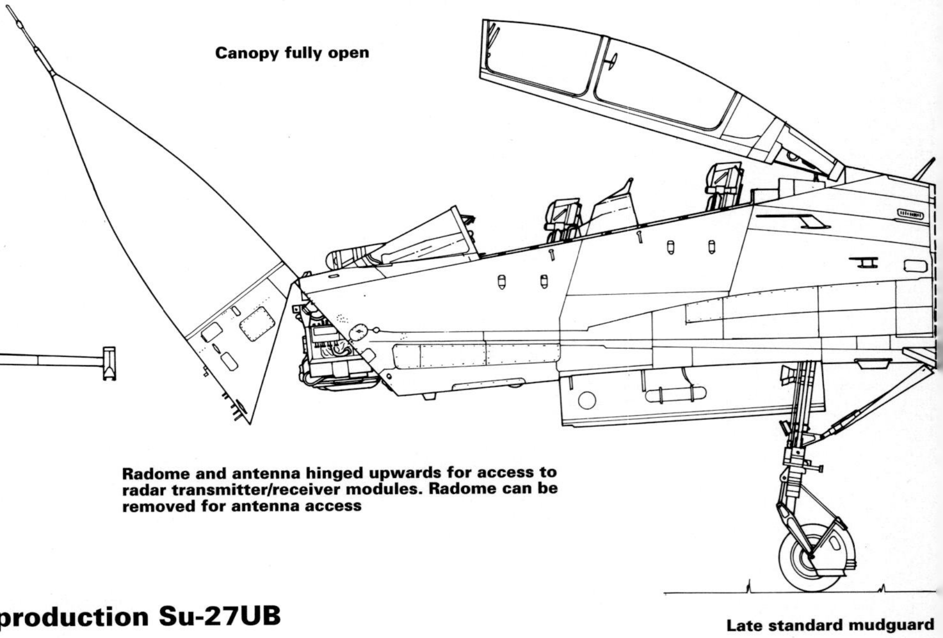

Radome and antenna hinged upwards for access to radar transmitter/receiver modules. Radome can be removed for antenna access

Late standard mudguard

Late production Su-27UB

Enlarged dorsal airbrake. Increased area necessary because maximum opening angle is smaller than on single-seat variants

Dielectric panel (ADF antenna?) further aft

Su-27UB retains full operational equipment, including radar

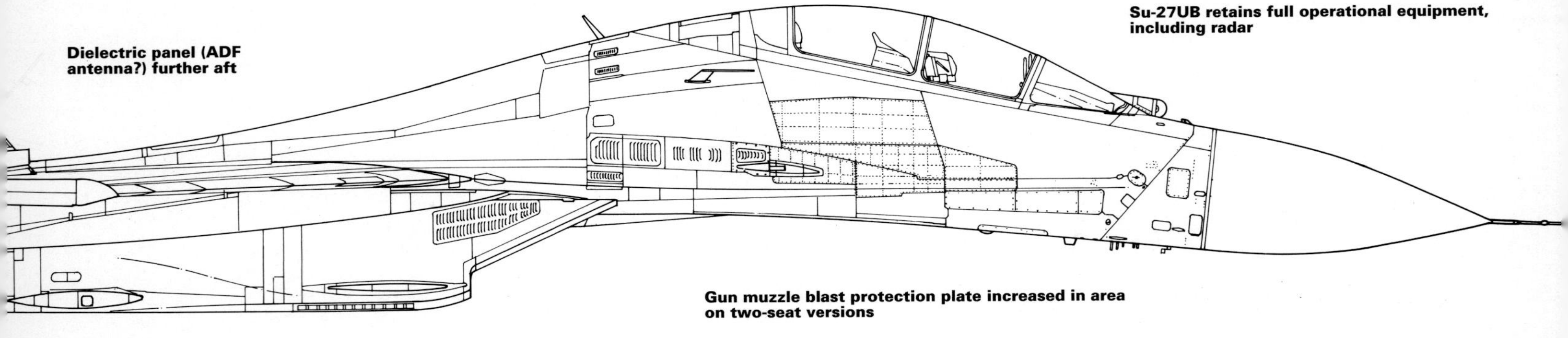

Gun muzzle blast protection plate increased in area on two-seat versions

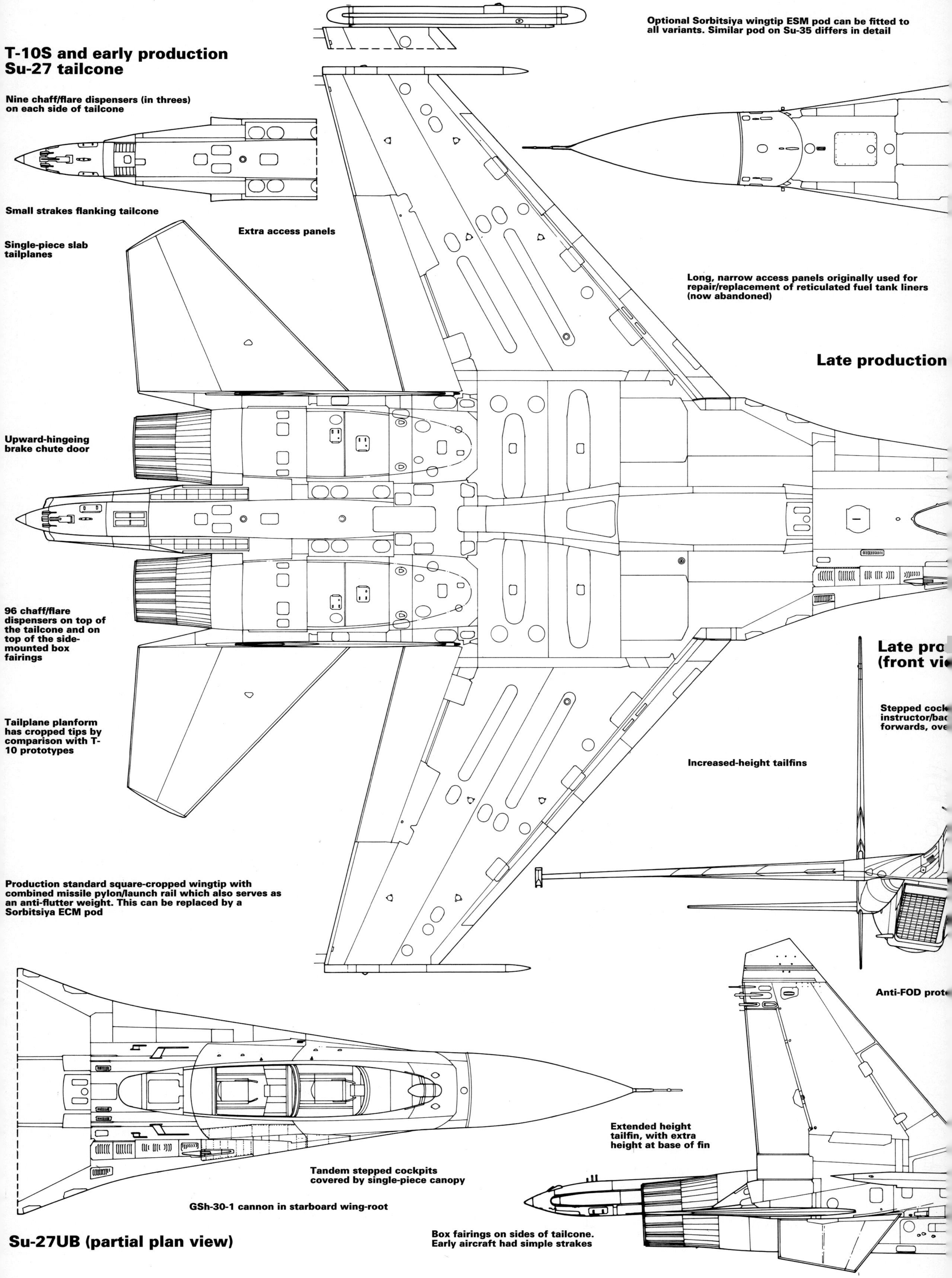
T-10S and early production Su-27 tailcone
Nine chaff/flare dispensers (in threes) on each side of tailcone
Small strakes flanking tailcone
Single-piece slab tailplanes
Extra access panels
Optional Sorbitsiya wingtip ESM pod can be fitted to all variants. Similar pod on Su-35 differs in detail
Long, narrow access panels originally used for repair/replacement of reticulated fuel tank liners (now abandoned)
Late production
Upward-hingeing brake chute door
96 chaff/flare dispensers on top of the tailcone and on top of the side-mounted box fairings
Late pro
(front vi
Stepped cock
instructor/bac
forwards, ove
Tailplane planform has cropped tips by comparison with T-10 prototypes
Increased-height tailfins
Production standard square-cropped wingtip with combined missile pylon/launch rail which also serves as an anti-flutter weight. This can be replaced by a Sorbitsiya ECM pod
Anti-FOD prot
Extended height tailfin, with extra height at base of fin
Tandem stepped cockpits covered by single-piece canopy
GSh-30-1 cannon in starboard wing-root
Su-27UB (partial plan view)
Box fairings on sides of tailcone. Early aircraft had simple strakes

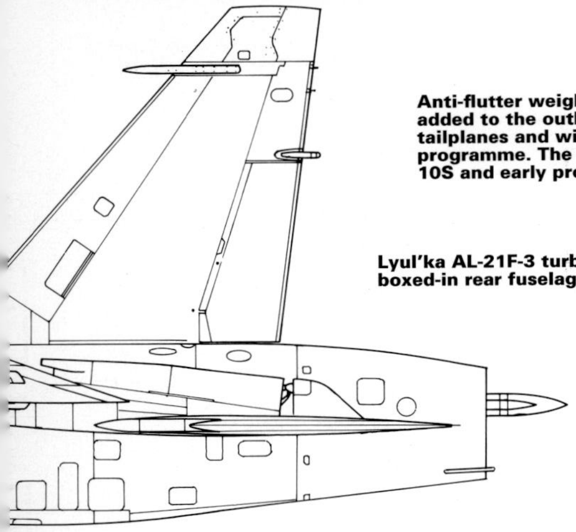

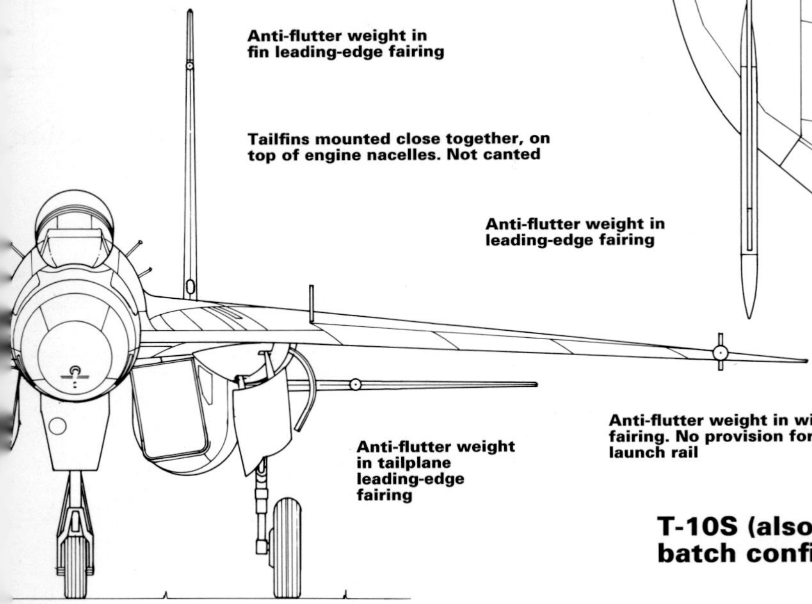

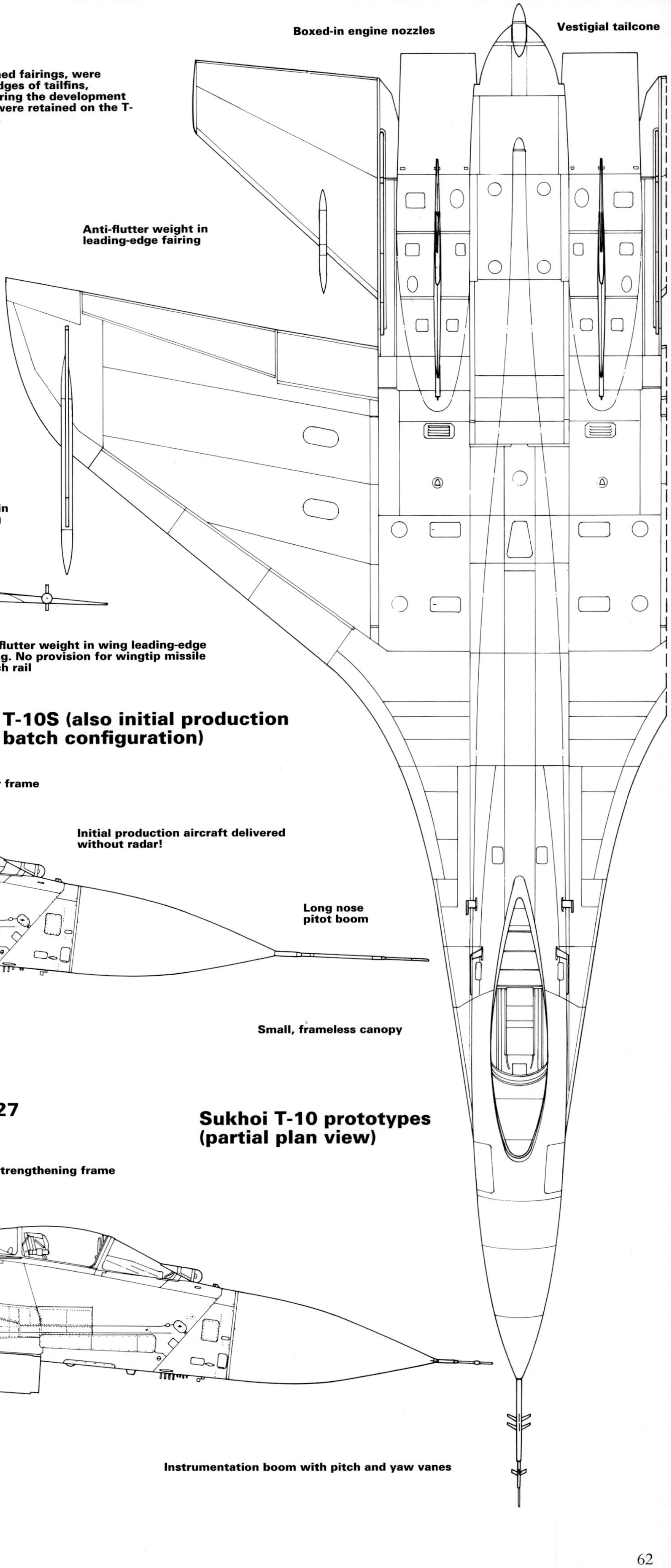

Sukhoi T-10 prototypes (partial plan view)

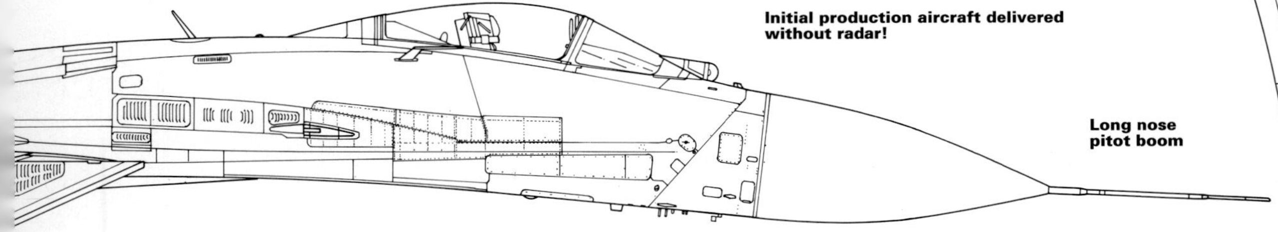

T-10S (also initial production batch configuration)

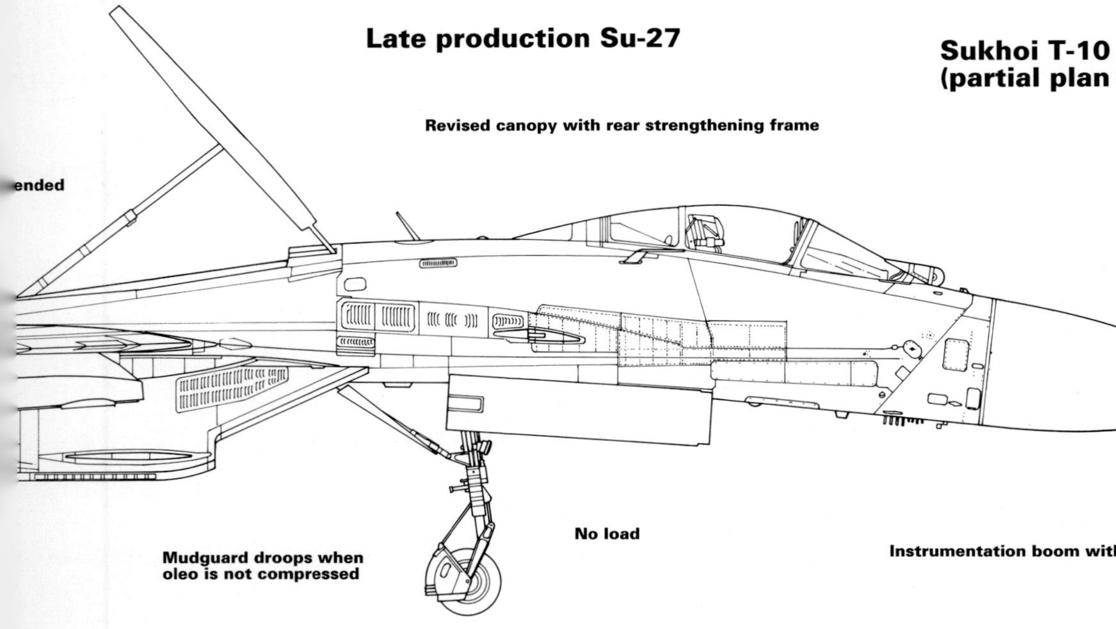

Late production Su-27

SCALE 1:72

1 2 3 Metres

1 2 3 4 5 6 7 8 9 10 Feet

Plans by Mark Styling, 1994

Su-27K (underside plan view)

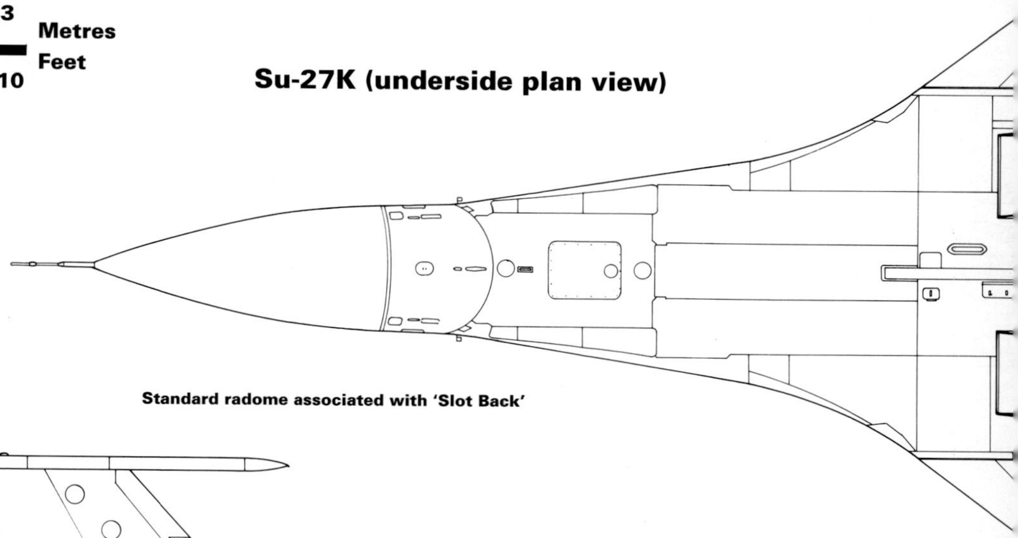

Standard pitot boom

Standard radome associated with 'Slot Back'

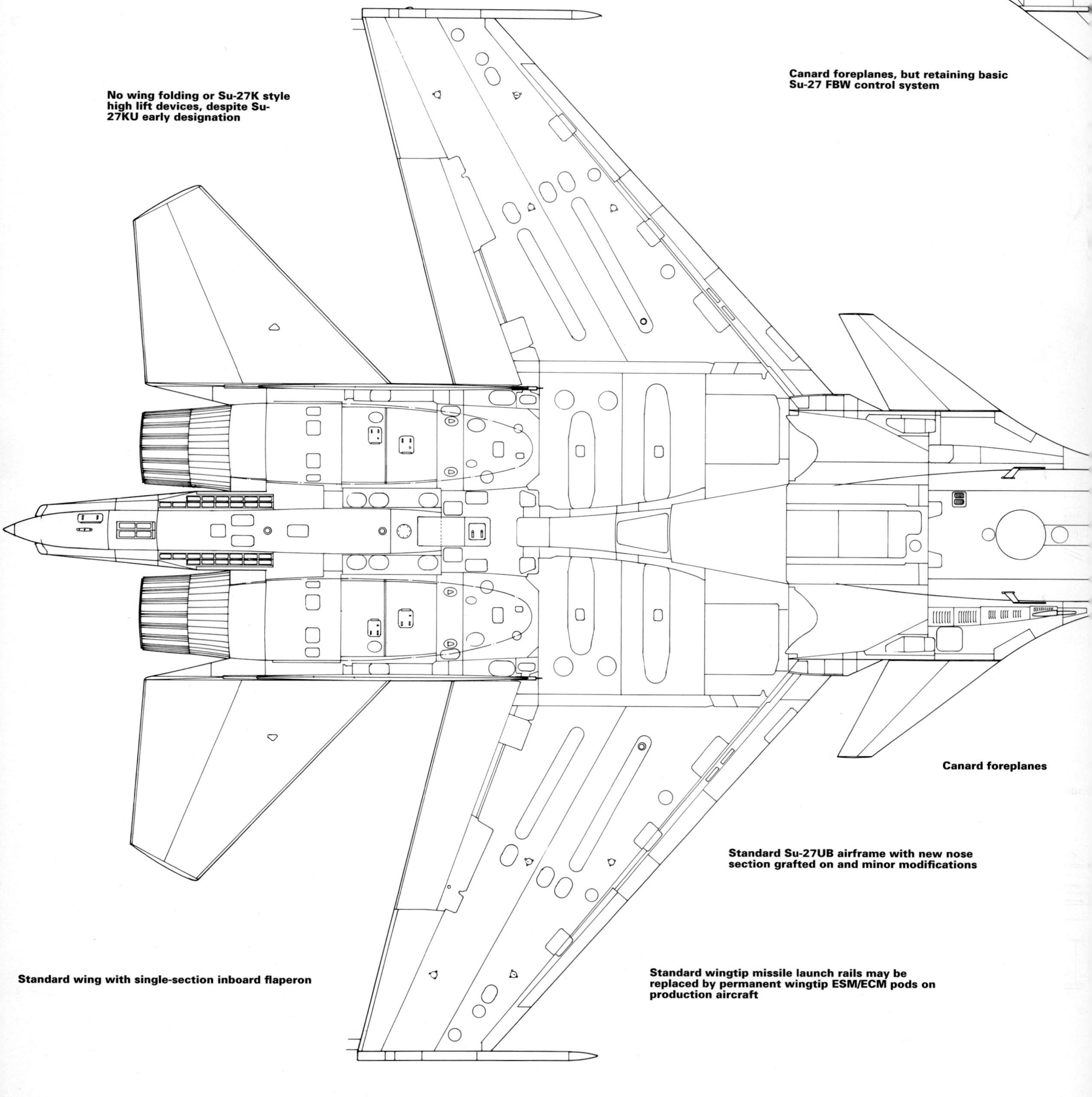

No wing folding or Su-27K style high lift devices, despite Su-27KU early designation

Canard foreplanes, but retaining basic Su-27 FBW control system

Canard foreplanes

Standard Su-27UB airframe with new nose section grafted on and minor modifications

Standard wing with single-section inboard flaperon

Standard wingtip missile launch rails may be replaced by permanent wingtip ESM/ECM pods on production aircraft

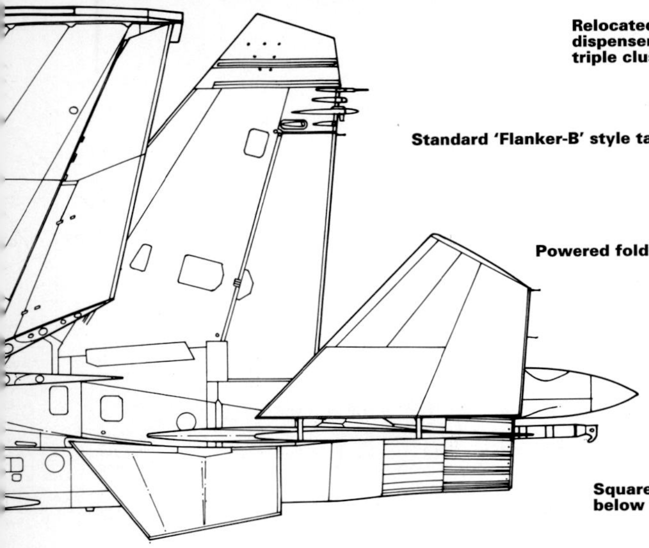

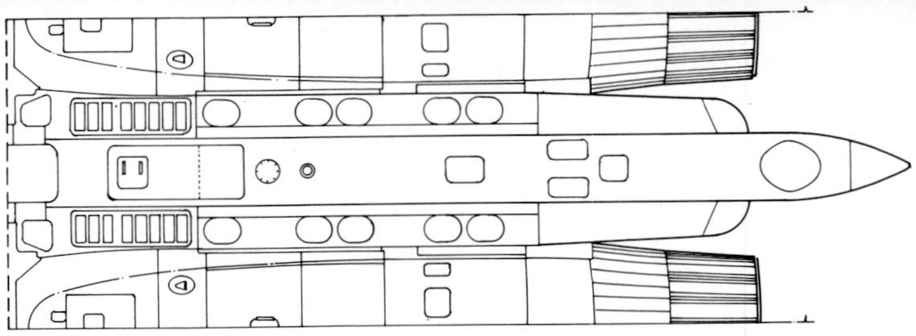

Su-27K (partial plan view)

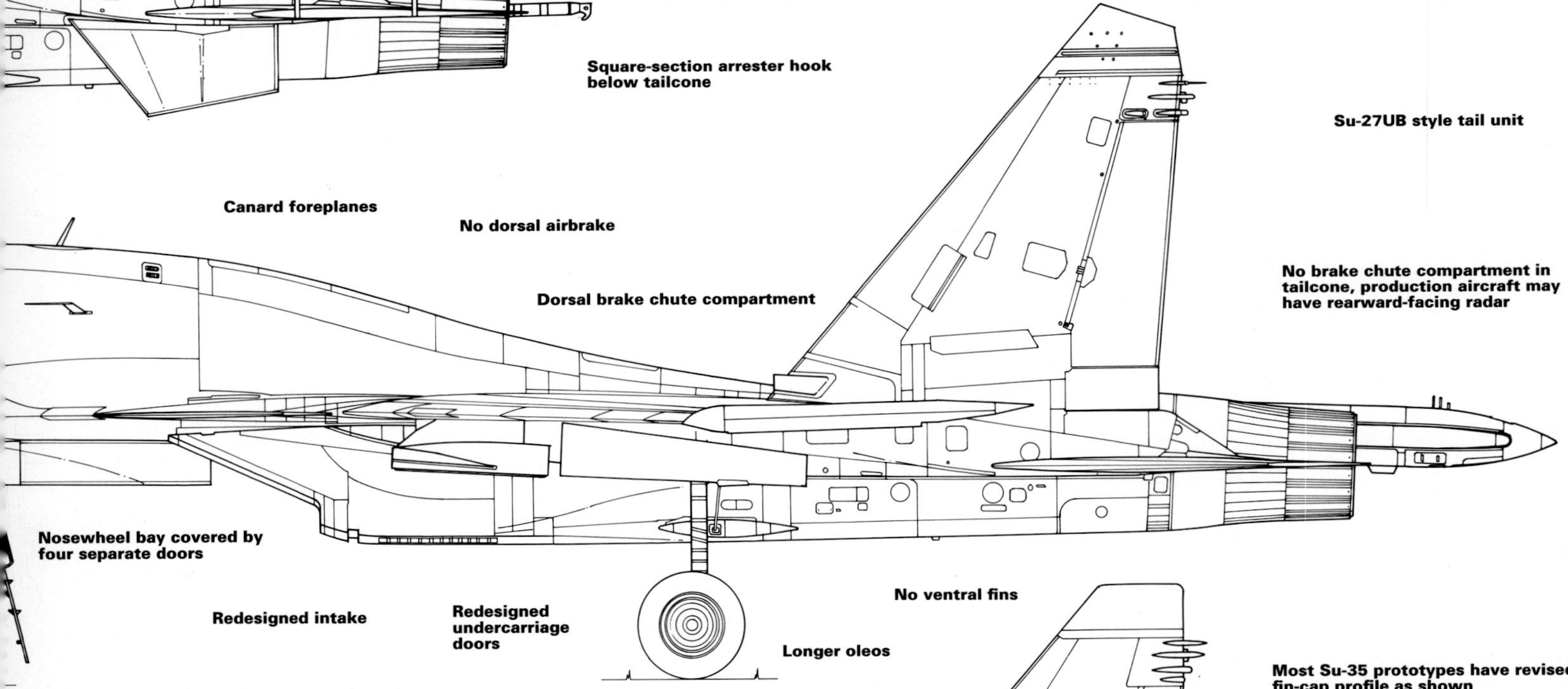

Su-27IB ('Su-34' prototype)

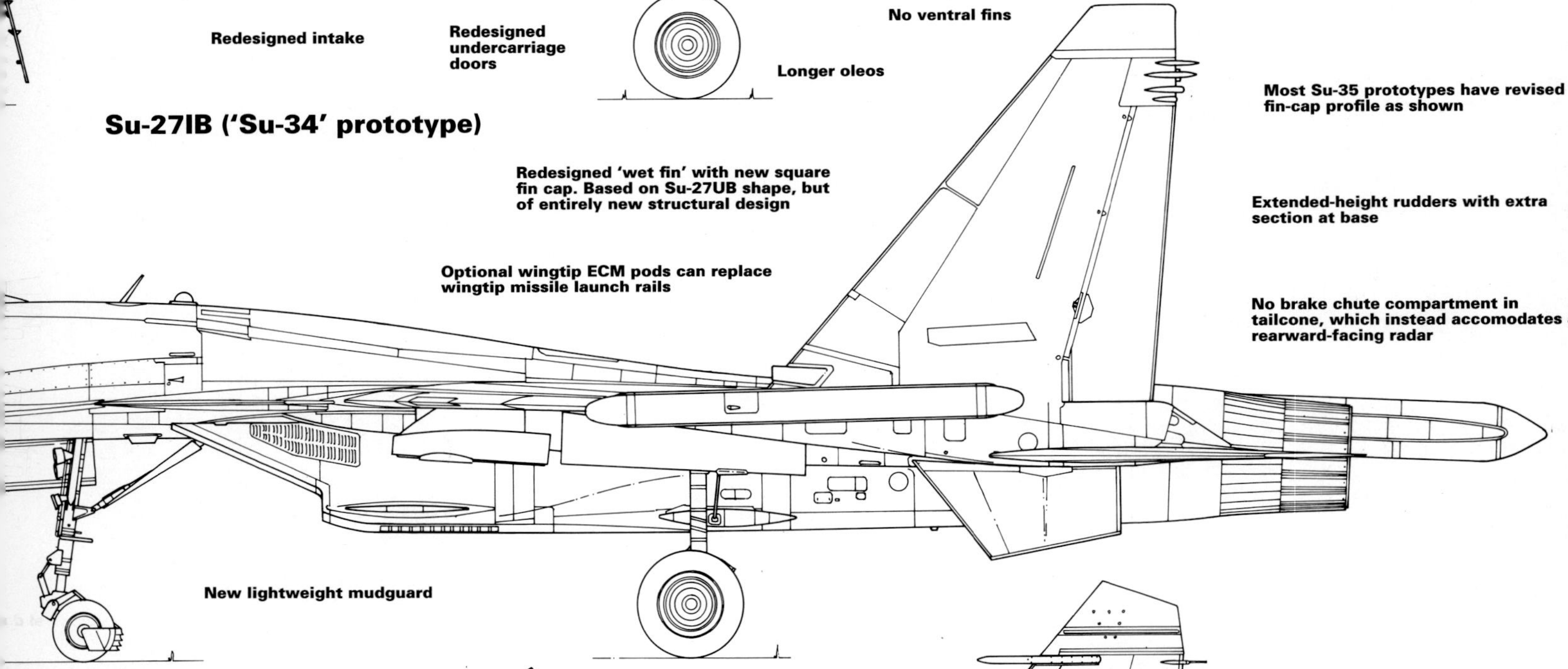

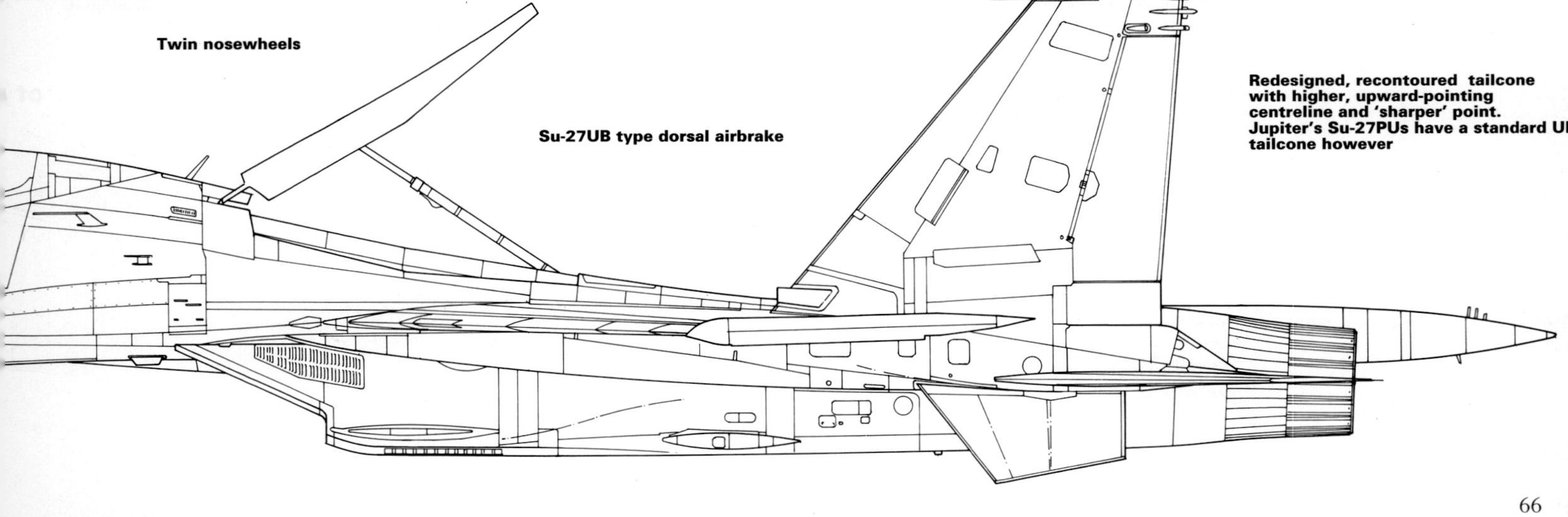

Su-27K (Su-33 prototype)

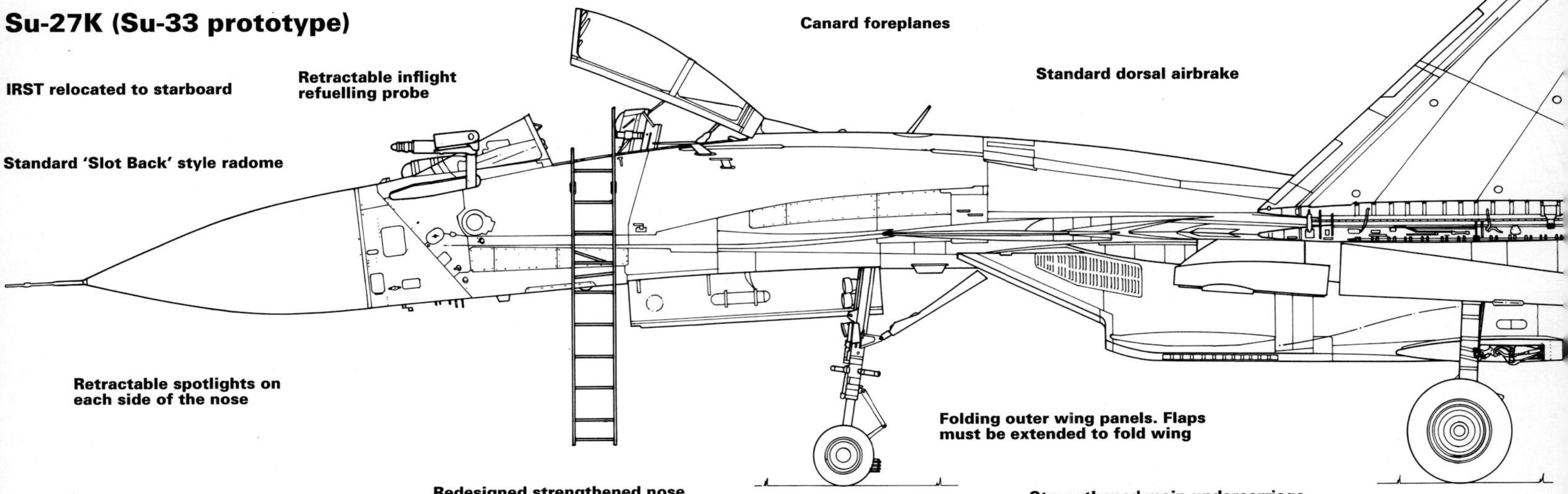

Su-27K (front view)

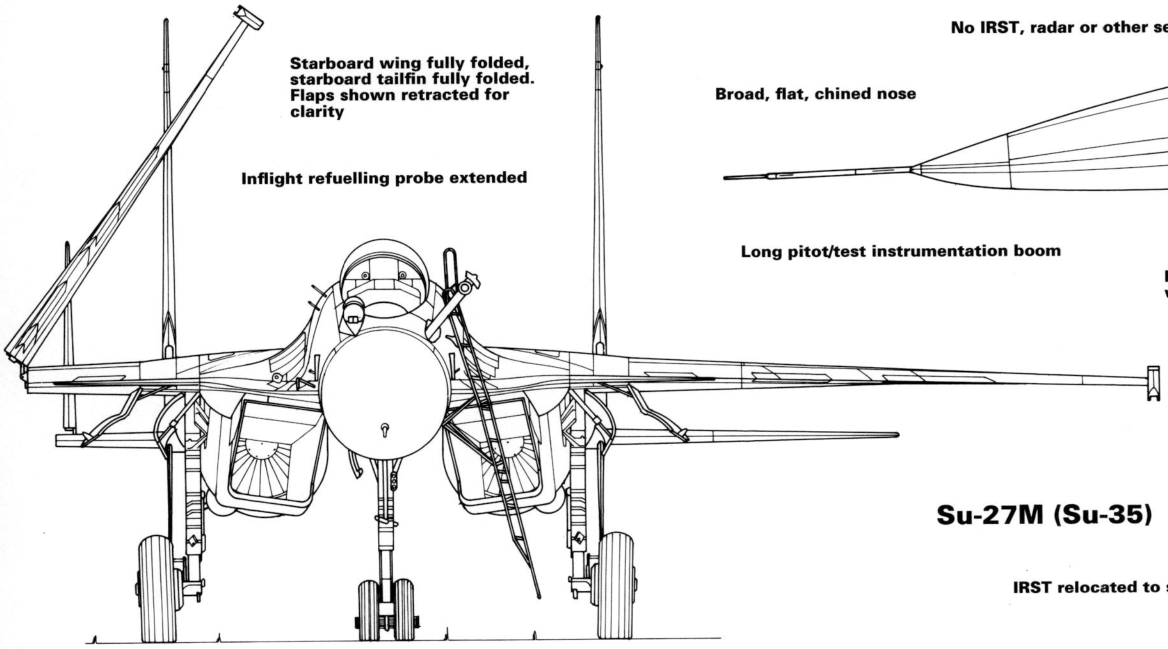

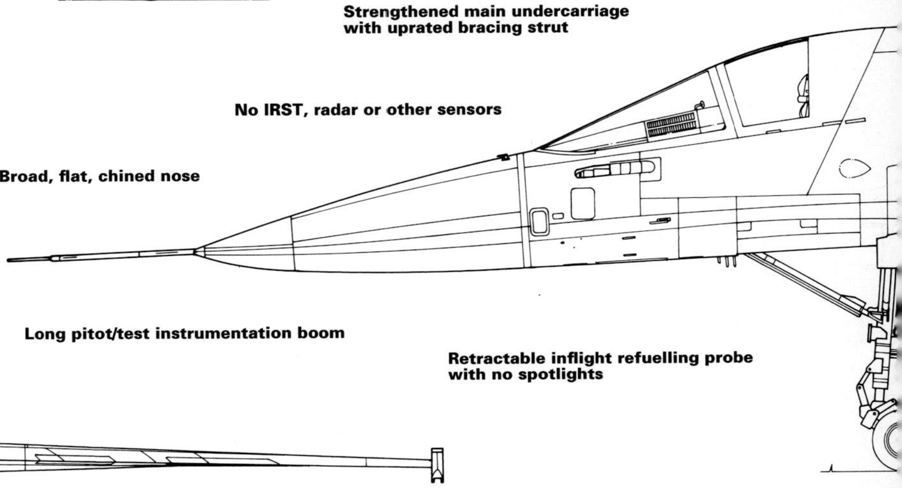

Su-27M (Su-35)

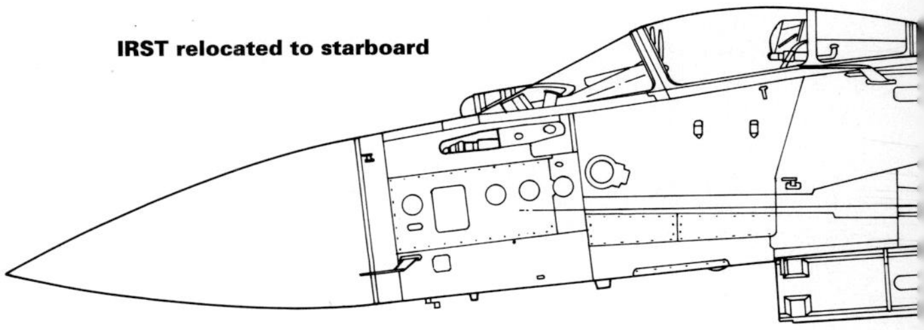

Su-27K (rear view)

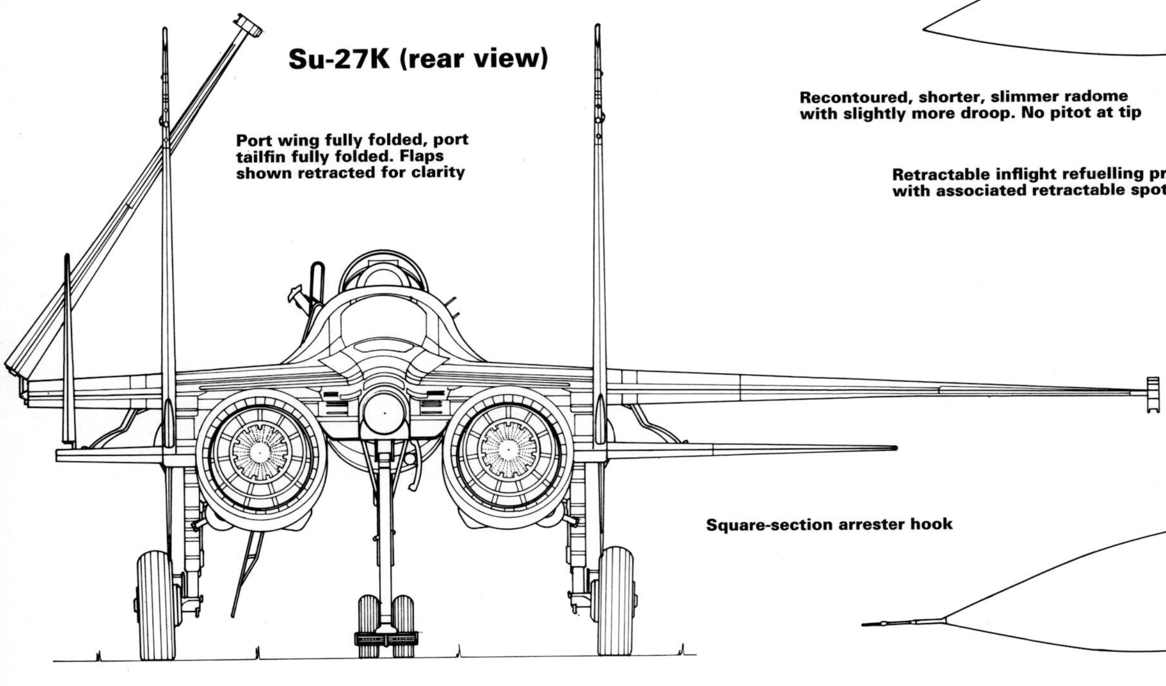

Su-27PU (Su-30 prototy

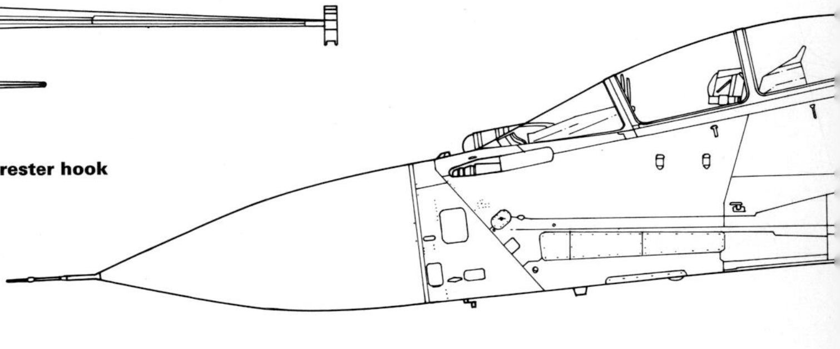

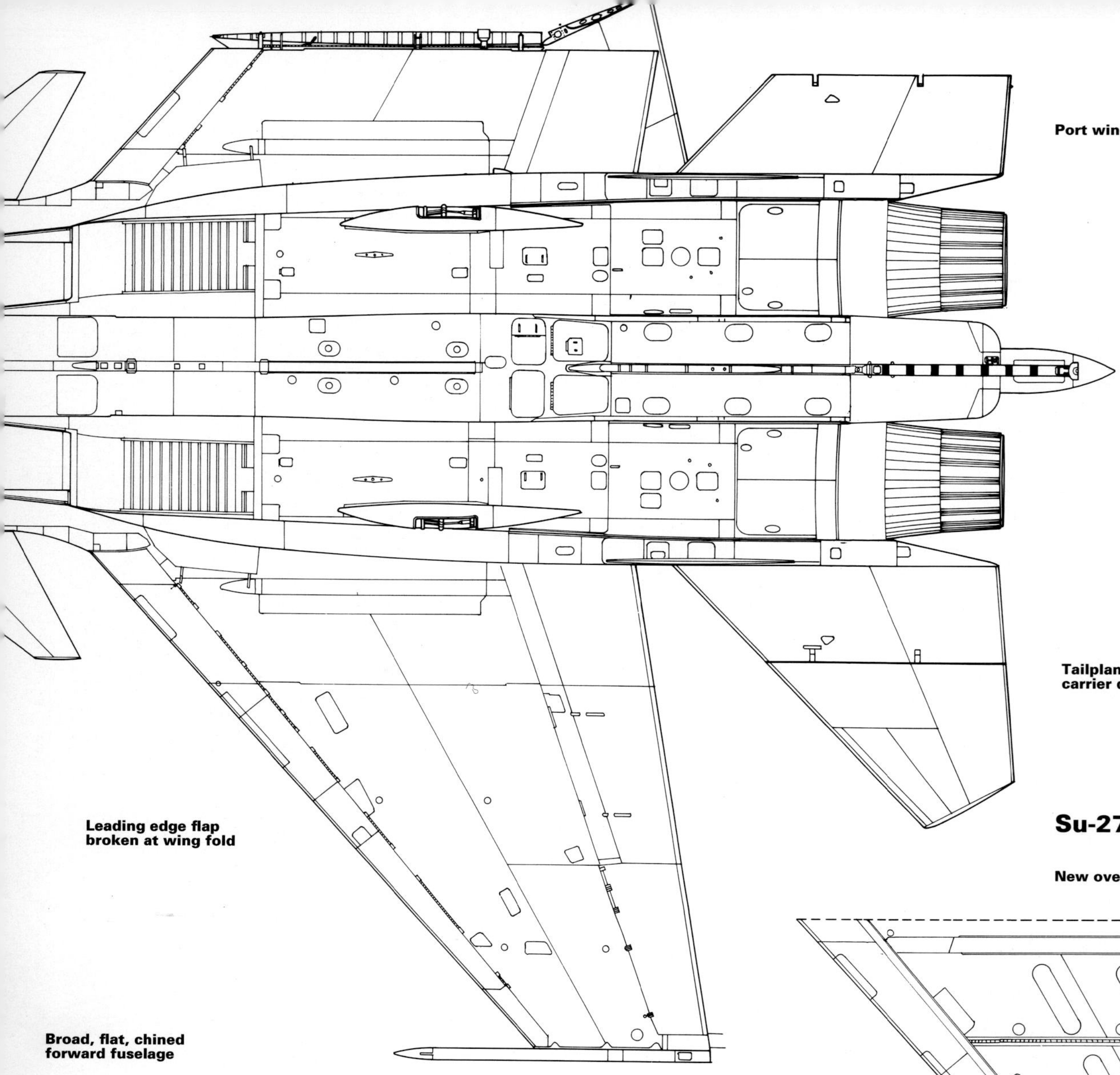

Port wing and tailplane shown folded

Square section arrestor hook beneath shortened tailcone

Tailplane folds to minimise space occupied on carrier deck or in hangar deck

Leading edge flap broken at wing fold

Su-27K (Topside of port wing)

New overwing fuel tank access panels

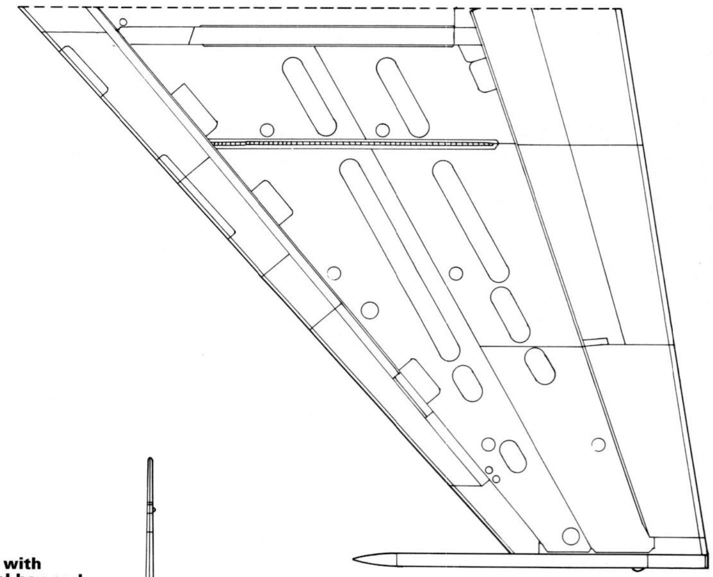

Outboard sections of three-section flaps function as drooping ailerons

Broad, flat, chined forward fuselage

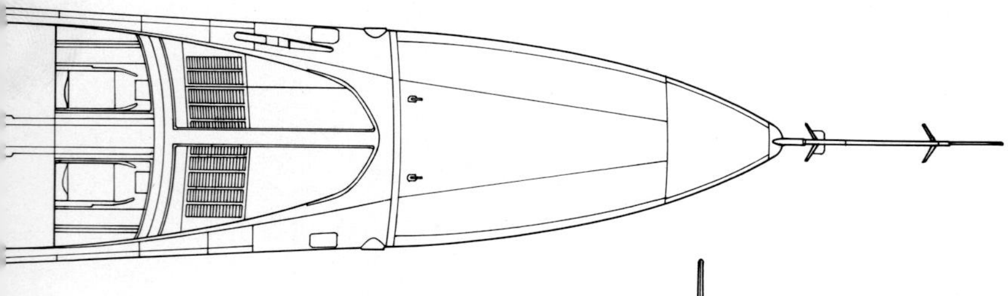

Su-27IB ('Su-34' prototype) topside plan view

New side-by-side cockpit with access through nosewheel bay and emergency egress only through roof panels

Retractable inflight refuelling probe

Strengthened undercarriage with longer oleos

Su-27IB ('Su-34' prototype) front view

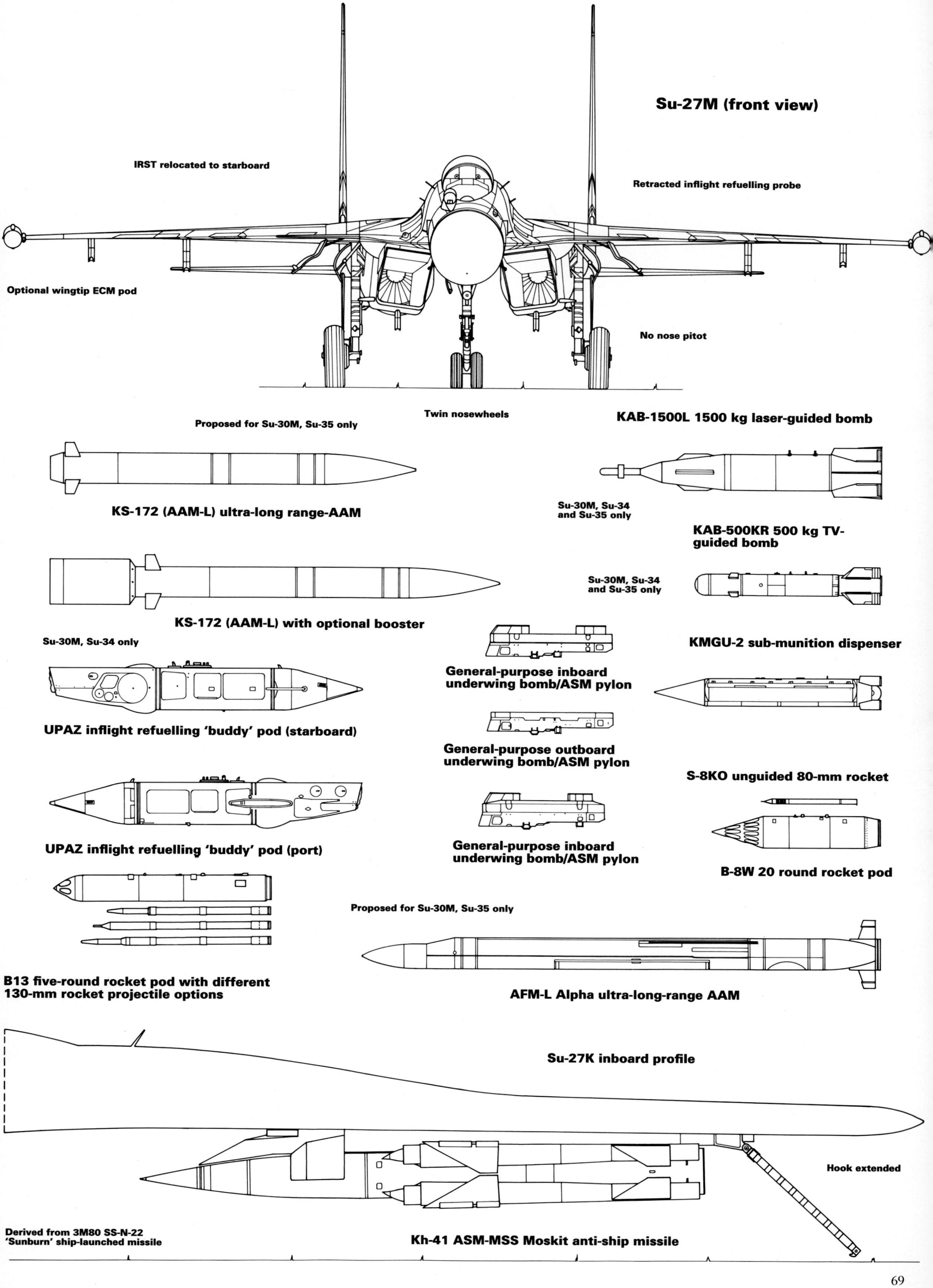
Su-27M (front view)
IRST relocated to starboard
Retracted inflight refuelling probe
Optional wingtip ECM pod
No nose pitot
Twin nosewheels
Proposed for Su-30M, Su-35 only
KAB-1500L 1500 kg laser-guided bomb
KS-172 (AAM-L) ultra-long range-AAM
Su-30M, Su-34
and Su-35 only
KAB-500KR 500 kg TV-
guided bomb
Su-30M, Su-34
and Su-35 only
KS-172 (AAM-L) with optional booster
Su-30M, Su-34 only
KMGU-2 sub-munition dispenser
General-purpose inboard
underwing bomb/ASM pylon
UPAZ inflight refuelling 'buddy' pod (starboard)
General-purpose outboard
underwing bomb/ASM pylon
S-8KO unguided 80-mm rocket
UPAZ inflight refuelling 'buddy' pod (port)
General-purpose inboard
underwing bomb/ASM pylon
B-8W 20 round rocket pod
Proposed for Su-30M, Su-35 only
B13 five-round rocket pod with different
130-mm rocket projectile options
AFM-L Alpha ultra-long-range AAM
Su-27K inboard profile
Hook extended
Derived from 3M80 SS-N-22
'Sunburn' ship-launched missile
Kh-41 ASM-MSS Moskit anti-ship missile

Configuration
The Su-27K/KU/IB configuration, with both tailplane and canards, is known to Sukhoi as an 'unstable triplane layout'. By destabilising the aircraft in pitch and providing control surfaces forward of the centre of gravity and centre of lift, canards improve manoeuvrability and counter the inevitable reduction of tailplane efficiency at high angles of attack.

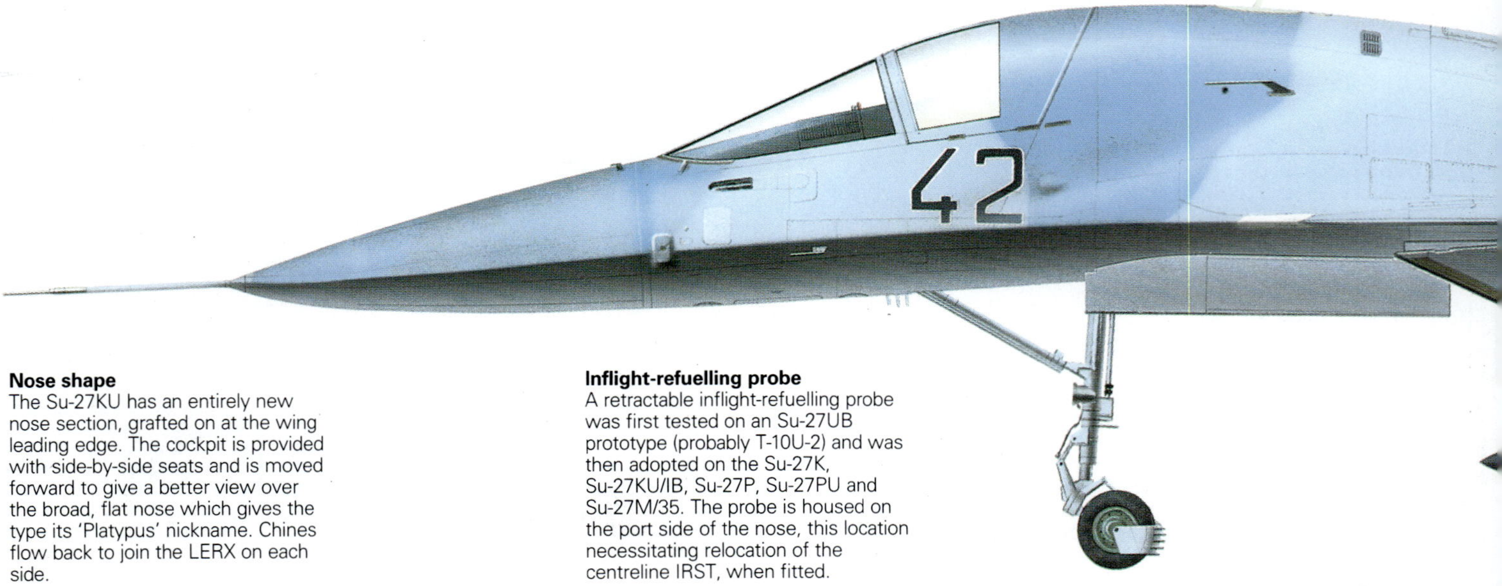

Nose shape
The Su-27KU has an entirely new nose section, grafted on at the wing leading edge. The cockpit is provided with side-by-side seats and is moved forward to give a better view over the broad, flat nose which gives the type its 'Platypus' nickname. Chines flow back to join the LERX on each side.

Inflight-refuelling probe
A retractable inflight-refuelling probe was first tested on an Su-27UB prototype (probably T-10U-2) and was then adopted on the Su-27K, Su-27KU/IB, Su-27P, Su-27PU and Su-27M/35. The probe is housed on the port side of the nose, this location necessitating relocation of the centreline IRST, when fitted.

Cockpit access
Access to the new side-by-side cockpit is via a ladder in the nosewheel bay, although the panels above the canopy look similar to the opening cockpit panels of the Su-24 'Fencer'.

Su-24 replacement
The Su-27IB is a potential 'Fencer' replacement, if funding permits.

Canard foreplanes
Canard foreplanes were first flown on the T-10-24 during May 1985, and were later selected for use on several advanced 'Flanker' variants, including the Su-27KU. These foreplanes improve take-off performance by generating extra lift forward of the centre of gravity, instead of generating a down force behind it like conventional tailplanes.

Sukhoi Su-27KU (Su-27IB?)

The Su-27KU (often referred to as the Su-27IB, and possibly designated T-10-42 by the OKB) is believed to have originated as a demonstrator/aerodynamic prototype for a carrierborne trainer for Su-27K pilots. It was first seen in a TASS photo approaching the carrier *Kuznetsov* (formerly *Tbilisi*) although it has no arrester hook, no wing or tailplane folding and no carrier equipment. The designation Su-27KU is the only one used by the Sukhoi OKB, the suffix 'KU' denoting carrier trainer. When displayed for CIS leaders at the closed air show at Minsk Maschulische in February 1992 the aircraft had an information board describing it as the Su-27IB (Istrebeitel, or fighter-bomber), and carried an impressive array of air-to-ground ordnance, although it lacked attack radar or any electro-optical sensors.

Undercarriage
The Su-27KU has a redesigned and strengthened undercarriage (probably based on the Su-27K landing gear), with longer oleos and a relocated rearward-retracting nosewheel, covered by four separate nosewheel doors.

Tailfins
The Su-27KU has the same increased height tailfins as those fitted to the Su-27UB, but surprisingly lacks ventral fins, despite its massive forward 'keel' area.

Armament
The aircraft is seen carrying R-73s outboard, and R-77 (AAM-M) AAMs furthest outboard. Underwing it carries a Kh-29L (port) or Kh-29T (starboard) with a KAB series LGB inboard and a Kh-31 ASM under each intake.

Wingtip launch rails
Most 'Flanker' sub-variants have wingtip missile launch rails which also serve as anti-flutter weights. Only the R-73 (AA-11 'Archer') has been seen on this pylon, though presumably similar lightweight missiles (like the R-60 AA-8 'Aphid') could also be carried. The pylons can quickly be replaced by cylindrical ECM pods.

INDEX

Picture acknowledgments

Front cover: Carey Schofield. **6-7:** Carey Schofield. **8:** Nigel Eastaway (two), Jon Lake. **9:** Robert J. Ruffle via Jon Lake. **11:** Royal Norwegian Air Force, via Jon Lake, Carey Schofield. **12:** Carey Schofield (three). **13:** Carey Schofield (two). **14:** Carey Schofield (three). **15:** Nigel Eastaway, Carey Schofield. **16:** Nigel Eastaway (two). **17:** Carey Schofield. **18:** Carey Schofield, via Jon Lake. **19:** Carey Schofield (two), Sergei Skrynnikov/AviaData. **21:** Jon Lake (seven), Nigel Eastaway. **22:** Joe Cupido (three), Jon Lake (four), David Donald. **27:** Jon Lake (two). **28:** David Donald (two). **29:** Jon Lake (four). **30:** David Donald (two). **31:** Jon Lake (three). **32:** David Donald, Jon Lake (two), Terry Senior. **33:** Jon Lake (two), Terry Senior, Sergei Skrynnikov/AviaData. **34:** via Jon Lake, A. Swanberg, Joe Cupido. **35:** Joe Cupido, Hughes. **36:** Martin Baumann, Hans Nijhuis (two). **37:** Hans Nijhuis (two), Jon Lake. **38:** Gert Kromhouts (two), Sergei Skrynnikov/AviaData. **39:** Nigel Eastaway. **40:** Jon Lake (two), Sergei Skrynnikov. **41:** Jon Lake (two), Sergei Skrynnikov. **42:** Jon Lake (six), Sergei Skrynnikov.**43:** Nigel Eastaway, via Simon Watson, Gerard Keysper. **44:** via Simon Watson, Gerard Keysper, Wojtek Matusiak via Jon Lake (two). **45:** Gerard Keysper, Jon Lake (three). **46:** Jon Lake (four). **47:** Hendrik J. van Broekhuizen, R. Holder. **48:** Jon Lake, TASS, Sukhoi via Jon Lake. **49:** Jon Lake (five). **50:** Carey Schofield. **51:** Jon Lake (two), Tim Senior. **54:** Sukhoi, Wojtek Matusiak (two). **55:** Sukhoi, Sergei Skrynnikov. **56:** Ian Black, Carey Schofield, Sergei Skrynnikov. **57:** Sukhoi, Jon Lake, Terry Senior, TASS, Avia-Data. **58:** Airshots, Jon Lake, Joe Cupido, David Donald. **59:** Sergei Popsuevich/AviaData (two), Sergei Skrynnikov/AviaData.